WHO SPEAKS FOR THE CHILD?

To Amy, Sarah, and Ann

WHO SPEAKS
FOR THE CHILD?

by

NORMAN E. SILBERBERG, PH.D.

Vice-President for Research and Education
Sister Kenny Institute
Minneapolis, Minnesota

and

MARGARET C. SILBERBERG, PH.D.

Psychological Consultant (Private Practice)
St. Paul, Minnesota

CHARLES C THOMAS • PUBLISHER
Springfield • Illinois • U.S.A.

Published and Distributed Throughout the World by
CHARLES C THOMAS • PUBLISHER
Bannerstone House
301-327 East Lawrence Avenue, Springfield, Illinois, U.S.A.

© *1974 by* CHARLES C THOMAS • PUBLISHER
ISBN 0-398-03014-6 (cloth)
ISBN 0-398-03015-4 (paper)
Library of Congress Catalog Card Number: 73-15509

*With THOMAS BOOKS careful attention is given to all details of
manufacturing and design. It is the Publisher's desire to present books
that are satisfactory as to their physical qualities and artistic possibilities and appropriate for their particular use. THOMAS BOOKS will
be true to those laws of quality that assure a good name and good will.*

Printed in the United States of America
Q-1

Library of Congress Cataloging in Publication Data

Silberberg, Norman E
    Who speaks for the child?

    1. Child study. 2. Intelligence levels. 3. Academic achievement.
I. Silberberg, Margaret C., joint author. II. Title.
LB1115.S65 1974   370.15   73-15509
ISBN O-398-03014-6
ISBN O-398-03015-4 (pbk.)

"I've *got* to protect them.
I'm bigger than they.

After all, a person's a person.
No matter how small."

Horton Hears a Who
— Dr. Seuss

CONTENTS

VII. TYPES OF BEHAVIOR PROBLEMS

VIII. ATTEMPTS TO CHANGE BEHAVIOR IN SCHOOL

WHO SPEAKS FOR THE CHILD?

CHAPTER I

HORROR STORIES

A 12-YEAR-OLD drives his teacher to exasperation. Finally, the teacher strikes the child on several occasions. Despite this, the child does not conform to scholastic demands placed upon him. The child is sufficiently depressed to raise the question of potential suicide. The child is evaluated psychologically and found to be mentally retarded, but never having been identified as such until that point. The child is placed in a special class, where the academic pressures are relieved, and the problem largely disappears.

A child is in special classes for the mentally retarded for several years. Finally, during a routine evaluation, someone suspects that the problems are somewhat different, and refers the child for an audiological evaluation. The child is not retarded, but is deaf.

A fourteen-year-old black child has been incarcerated in three different detention centers for truancy over the past three years. In each case, persons connected with one of the governmental agencies dealing with such problems imply to the mother that there are no options. The mother becomes very unhappy because the child wants to live with his family and does not want to learn the types of things that they teach him in the detention centers. Finally, after all of this suffering, the mother is put in touch with Legal Aid.

A married couple adopted four children. As they grew, it became evident that one had problems which could probably be attributable to neurological causes. The child is hyperactive, impulsive, and destructive. This type of behavior often responds well to medication. Instead, the school sent the family to a community agency where family therapy is invoked. The result of

3

this therapy is such that the parents are currently talking of divorce, while the four children continue to be torn by the ambiguity of the therapy situation. In the meantime, the brain-damaged child continues to be hyperactive, impulsive, and destructive.

An extremely bright twelve-year-old girl is a source of distress to the school. Although it is known that she is an excellent student, she does not conform to the academic demands placed upon her. She is evaluated and found to have such poor fine motor coordination that she cannot do extended writing tasks. This particular school insists on long workbook assignments every day. It takes two years of communication between an outreach worker and the school before the school is willing to alter its program sufficiently to allow the child a minimum writing load. The behavior problems disappear.

An eight-year-old Indian child is removed from his family by welfare and is placed in a foster home. On several occasions he runs away from the foster home and finds his way back to his natural family. Each time he is returned. The initial crime was truancy. When it is pointed out to the welfare department that this child is unable to read efficiently and the school is making unfair demands upon him in reading, it is then recommended that he be returned to his family. A psychologist works with the school to help design a more realistic academic program for this child, whose truancy is reduced significantly.

A young man has a great deal of difficulty reading. Nevertheless, he entered college and was given a flexible program based on some of the ideas proposed in this book. With this help, he gets through four years of college with a 1.98 average (C is 2.00). He gets a job as a counselor working with youth, which was appropriate for him because he is very sensitive to the needs of children. But his college balked at giving him the diploma, because he just missed his C average. Because he does not have a degree, he is in danger of losing his job.

At a night club some years ago, the attendant in the lady's room was sitting reading a book in French. It turned out she had a Master's degree in education, but she could not get a job in that city. She was black.

A social studies text book deals with the Sioux Indians in one paragraph. It tells that they existed by stealing from their neighbors. An Indian boy is asked "Who discovered America?" and answers "Columbus."

A parent goes to visit a school for children with learning difficulties. It is very quiet and orderly. This is interrupted by a child being dragged down the hall screaming to the "time out" room. They remove his belt and shoelaces and lock him in the padded room. The parent cries.

A ninth grade child locks himself in the closet and refuses to go to school. He is called emotionally disturbed. He is evaluated — after nine years of misery — and it is found that he reads at the first grade level. After changing his program according to his strengths, he returns to school and begins to adjust. He still cannot read because he confuses the directions that letters face. He is frightened of physical education because he is always going the wrong way and getting hurt. His teacher will not excuse him from physical education.

An immature child is having some difficulties adjusting to his second grade classroom. The teacher calls his sixth grade sister down from her room. She stands in the front of the room while the teacher calls on children in the class to tell about all the bad things her brother does in class.

A parent is concerned because his son is doing below-average work in the class. He drags his son from clinic to clinic to find out how to get his son to be a good student. He goes through all kinds of expensive "cure" programs. The only effect of these cures is to convince the child that he is a freak.

A high school locks the children in and gives them only spoons in the lunch room. The school has a substantial number of minority children. The next school over has more minority children but is more free and easy in the way they treat them. The second school has fewer disruptions.

A child is seen by a psychologist who finds that the boy has low potential for school. A psychiatrist talks briefly to the boy, decides he is normal, and puts the parents into therapy.

A father goes into a rage because his son in junior high school is doing so poorly in school and breaks his son's arm. The boy *is then* tested and found to be borderline mentally retarded.

There are more horror stories in the following chapters. These stories, and the ones above, are some of those known personally to us. There are some worse, but the idea should be clear by now.

These stories are horror stories because of ignorance and intolerance. We hope to help this situation with this book.

CHAPTER II

APOLOGY

THIS HANDBOOK IS designed to summarize certain information about children who attend school. We do not intend it to be a textbook, but rather a handbook to use as reference for some facts about children and their schooling.

It is hoped that it will be factual without being dull and amusing without being facetious. There will be some bias in the writing because all writers (and most people) are biased.

We hope we are biased in favor of children and teachers because we feel both groups need all the warm support they can get. They have too long been the scapegoat for those myths in society which do not work out.

This chapter is in the form of an apology. In classic writings, plays led off with an apology, which was not an "I'm sorry" statement, but rather was a statement of the author's position so the audience could better understand what came later.

Again and again, as you read this book, you will note that there is only one thing that we can say for sure about children, and that is "they are all different." As a matter of fact, we really cannot talk about *children,* but about this child or that child.

In education and in psychology, we tend to group children under certain labels. Most books seem to aim at unlocking the genius hidden in the child classified in a certain way, whether it be learning disabled, retarded, gifted, or any other type. This has led to a great deal of pressure on the child, his parents, and the teacher.

The main problem about this approach is that in some cases, not all information is given out to the public (including the teachers), while in other cases misinformation is given.

In this book, we are attempting to fill in that information

gap. We feel that, if a parent, teacher, and child all knew what to expect from each other, they would be able to deal with each other more effectively and more affectionately. Possibly, there would be less of a need to call in outside help. It is for this reason that we are trying to explain concepts which seem to blow the minds of our audiences, such as why 50 percent of children must read below grade level, that many "abnormal" school behaviors are quite normal, that "the apple doesn't fall far from the tree," that organized sports may do more harm than good, and that it is ridiculous to think about college as it now is for most children.

These ideas are based on facts. In presenting some unusual facts, one is tempted to back it up with references, involving footnotes and more extensive descriptions of studies. We have mentioned some books and articles in our writing, some of which are listed in the bibliography at the end. These should be a good starting point for the reader who wants to dig further.

But this is not the purpose of this book. Hopefully, many of the thoughts put forth will challenge the reader to at least think about the rightness or wrongness of what we say. The facts presented will be hard for some people to handle, because many parents and teachers take *too much* responsibility for how their children turn out. These people may call us pessimists. We do not agree. We feel that we should face reality as often as possible instead of continuing to build our lives on the fluffy myths that constitute much of educational thought. It is only by being realistic that we can be fair to our children.

This book is aimed at being a reference book for parents and teachers. Almost every child in our society is described someplace in this book. But we must caution you against reading *all* the things described into one child.

By trying to do an overview of school learning and behavior problems, while touching on the home and street, we necessarily have to be superficial at times. For example, we discuss individual differences in a few pages, while entire texts are devoted to the subject. In other places, we give our opinion of what is going on or as to what to do, without giving equal time to some other views. This is because there are often so many other views that we do not have time and space for it.

Many others also have opinions that are critical of education and child rearing. Most of these are well-meaning and based on a solid basis of information. But all too often these critics want basically the same thing as they are criticizing, but only done in a different way. They all seem to fall in a category that we call "How I Blew My Students' Minds And Interested Them In Reading, Writing, and Arithmetic." Another group is interested in having schools be a pleasant place — at any cost. These are the ones where Yoga, sight-seeing, and knot-tying have been raised to the status of major subjects in school. We are not against children learning about these things in school, although often we feel that many of these nonpractical interests of students could better be taught in storefront schools, churches, community centers, etc. But when a child has no idea about what the first amendment to the Constitution says, we cannot get very turned on if, thanks to their school, they can make a pretty wallhanging.

In other cases, cults have been built around certain educational ideas and we get our personal kicks at punching holes in the "logic" of some of these cults. In any case, we are latecomers in the opinion-giving game. Many expensive and painful educational plans are built, not on facts, but on opinions. We like to think that our opinions are at least based on fact, rather than on tradition, fad, or the marketing needs of textbook publishers.

We can, in fact, summarize our opinions in the idea that we are trying to be advocates for the child. We feel we can best do this by getting unrealistic pressures off the child, while converting the energies of parents and teachers into attempting to change education so that school becomes an appropriate, pleasant and successful experience for more children. This may mean taking a look at the whole educational process and changing it radically.

We are not so smug that we feel we can give the best direction on how these changes should take place. It will be seen in this book that we feel that education spends much too much time with "how" we teach children, rather than trying to figure out "what" to teach children. We have tried to give some suggestions on "what", realizing that there is so much brain power among parents and teachers that they should be able to figure out "how" better than we can.

We have not neglected writing on "how" we teach. There are now so many books and government supported programs designed to get children to conform and achieve above grade level, that we felt one dissenting voice should be thrown into that confusion. Certainly, we hope that these other programs are as willing as we are to defend our position.

But we are seldom asked to defend our position. It is interesting, but we have written quite a few articles lately which attack the myths of education at least as strongly as we do here. Parts of our chapter on sports appeared on the sports page of a newspaper. Our attempts to show that remedial reading does not work have appeared in journals for professional educators. We have attacked the misuse of achievement tests before large audiences. And hardly anybody argued with us, even though they kept right on doing the same thing we are attacking. We attacked the government's "Right to Read" program in a well-read journal (we asked for the right to learn), and the government recently increased the size of their expenditures for this program. We cited research showing that remedial reading does not work, and several local school districts increased their monies for remedial reading. We attacked behavior modification as an infringement on human rights, and the programs grew. We blamed our society's unrealistic demands for academic conformity for many cases of juvenile delinquency, so they brought police into the schools (to cut out the middle man in arrests?).

Possibly, talking to academicians is not the right way. In this book, we are talking to parents and teachers. Many of you will, hopefully, ask after finishing this book, "What can we do?" Our answer is to subvert from within. Changes must come first on a local level. If several school districts start a bookless program, a major publisher will package a curriculum to sell those districts but, in the meantime, they will sell other districts on such a program as well. Within the school, be nicer to the children and, when they get home, make them realize that you, too, believe they had a hard day. Elect people to the school board who are more interested in children than they are in budgets. Try to start a program where the superintendent of schools has to occasionally step into a classroom or talk to a student or teacher. Tell your children to take pride in themselves. Let them know that they and other children are valuable and important. Provide an example of treating children like humans instead of acting in a way that W. C. Fields implied (when asked in one movie whether he liked children, he replied "If they're well-done, yes").

Remember that your goals have to be realistic, too. You may not like a child, even if he is your own child or your student, just as you may not like your neighbor. You may not be able to do many of the things we suggest because of your own hang-ups. Some ideas may cause you pain (We remember one school administrator saying to us, after we had suggested some ideas for his school, "In my heart I know you are right, but in my guts I know that learning should not be fun.") But if you can face this, and say it, it may make life for those around you a little more pleasant.

Some may read this and feel that our approach is too permissive. We disagree. We describe it as a humanistic approach. This means that there should be kindness toward children, but that they must be allowed some responsibility for their own actions. Parents often spend too much time lecturing and scolding their children. This approach can develop a selective deafness in the child, rather than improve their behavior. It's like the old Jewish tale of two brothers, one devout and the other an atheist. The devout one worked and prayed but was poor. The atheist ignored prayer but was successful. Finally, the devout one raised his eyes to heaven and asked, "Oh Lord, why have you ignored me for so long?" And the voice boomed back from above, "Because you *bug* me too much!"

But we feel children will be willing to take more responsibility for their own actions if we give them a chance, instead of always saying to them, "Do it my way". We must admit that, despite all our wisdom of years, we have not done such a great job with the world. If we give the young a chance, they surely cannot do much worse.

This book is intended for general information. This means that we hope that you will learn enough from it so that you do not have to go elsewhere for help. For this reason, it does not deal with problems which are a matter of legality. Whether something is illegal or not is often a problem in the society which needs more effort than can be given in the face to face dealings of parent or teacher and child.

This may be seen by some as a cop-out. In this book we talk very little of the problem behaviors which eventually become most important as the child grows older, which are drugs, alcohol, and sex. But these are behaviors which are written about in other contexts much more fully than we can here. We are not sure that these problems would be so great if there were less pressure on these children to succeed in school and conform to unrealistic standards for behavior. Questions about the legalization of marijuana and heroin, restrictions of liquor and beer advertising, and the availability of abortions and birth control devices require the opinions of economists, sociologists, citizen representatives, urban planners, as well as psychologists. We decided to stick to what we know best.

For this reason, we are dealing with school aged children. Although our interest includes all school aged children, we are tending to emphasize a special group. This group was described by Thomas Jefferson in 1783, in his plan for public education:

> These schools to be under a visitor, who is annually to chuse the boy, of best genius in the school, of those whose parents are too poor to give them further education, and to send him forward to one of the grammar schools, of which twenty are proposed to be erected in different parts of the country, for teaching Greek, Latin, geography, and the higher branches of numerical arithmetic. Of the boys thus sent in any one year, trial is to be made at the grammar schools one or two years, and the best genius of the whole selected and continued six years, and the residue dismissed. By this means twenty of the best geniuses will be raked from the rubbish annually, and be instructed, at the public expense, so far as the grammar schools go.

It is this "rubbish" that we are emphasizing. Throughout our history, we have talked of equality but acted in such a way that we have selected out a small group to be the good, rich, white elite, while we left the rest as rubbish. We feel that it is time that society, including parents, teachers, and the children themselves stop seeing children who are not tops in school as rubbish. It is time we look at all children and realize that we have far too long been throwing too many on the trash heap.

This requires an advocacy for children.

For years, persons who served children did so based on the "Medical Model." This means that we viewed children who were in trouble behaviorally or scholastically as sick. We tried to cure them of their sickness but, in fact, we were trying to cure them of being themselves. We attached "sick" names, like "neurotic" or "emotionally disturbed," to such children. Books were written to define different types of sicknesses.

The "Advocacy Model" is much simpler. Except for the very few children whose behavior is so far out as to be a danger to themselves or others, we define our problem child as one who *bothers* someone with power. This child may bother his teacher by not reading well, he may bother his parents by being active at home, he may bother the police by standing on the corner and being black, he may bother the social worker because he is not being raised in a God-fearing middle class home, etc.

The Advocacy Model looks first at these sources of power. Before we can call a child sick, we must look at those institutions where he bothers someone to see if, given a change in that institution, he would not be a bother anymore. For example, in the case of the child with "an emotional block" in reading, we can cure him of his sickness simply by having the school find other ways to teach him.

This is what the child's advocate does. Let us give an example:

Interestingly, when you get into why most children bother someone in power, you find one strange thing happening over and over. It turns out that usually it is not the child's behavior that is bothering someone, but rather the *age* at which that behavior shows up which causes the problems. In other words, it is not that a child reads poorly or is overactive, because we expect four-year-olds to read poorly or be overactive. It is the fact that the child is over four years of age which causes the problem.

Sometimes we think that if we could hide a child's age from parents and teachers, the child wouldn't bother them so much. But rather than wasting effort to try to get the child to read, or to slow down in their activity level, the advocate may try to explain individual differences to the parent and teacher. He may explain that all children grow at different rates and that what we call "average" only represents the behavior which can only be achieved by 50 percent of children that age. Sometimes, by doing this, the child doesn't bother them so much, and is not a problem anymore.

It is time to speak for the child.

Some of the things said in this book are in direct opposition to the views that prevail in newspapers, professional books, state departments of education, etc. The most common arguments against our views that we hear are the following:

1) "We know of one child who was in that program that you say does not work and it did wonders for him."

Response: (a) Are you sure that it worked? (b) Even if true, is it worth it? We are sure that the Spanish Inquisition really allowed a few people to truly find God. But was it worth killing and torturing the rest for the sake of the few?

2) "We have never seen these kinds of bad things happen in our school."

Response: We have. Maybe someplace "out there" it doesn't, but those people are so happy they'll never see this book anyway.

3) "If none of this stuff works, why am I doing it? I have to believe it works."

Response: How about trying something different?

4) "As the twig is bent, so shall it grow."

Response: (a) Kids are not twigs. (b) This is usually interpreted as meaning we need super controls.

5) "I believe in what you say, but we still have to live in the real world."

Response: We see very little in the real world that convinces us it doesn't need change.

6) "What you say may be true, what about my child today?"

Response: This is our weakest argument. We can talk of change and the hope that things may get better for that child before he finishes school, but there certainly is not a groundswell for change today. Our fear is that most changes are a holding action, designed to keep the *status quo* with as little give as possible. The only way to bring about real change is to start from the bottom.

Parents and teachers must argue for change. They must demand that schools, professionals, and government agencies do not continue to deal with children in terms of their own administrative convenience, but that they must work for children. Parent and teacher groups must change from passive social groups into advocacy agencies. Since many teachers are also parents, it may be best for them to work from this status rather than jeopardizing their jobs.

We must stop blaming teachers for the individual differences present in all children. Instead of being guardians of the bulletin board and lunchroom monitors, they must be allowed to teach. Teachers must become involved in curriculum building, instead of depending upon the skills of the textbook salesman in that district. Schools and home must become an exciting and challenging place. Parents and teachers must no longer war, but work together for the benefit of the child.

We are not saying in this book that all children are interesting, kind, and warm little humans. Rather, we are pleading for a chance for them to do well or poorly as human beings on their own, rather than forcing some into the latter category.

CHAPTER III

IQ AND ACHIEVEMENT

INDIVIDUAL DIFFERENCES — WHAT PSYCHOLOGY IS ALL ABOUT

CHILDREN ARE PEOPLE. Because they are people, they are all different and special. At any given age, they come in all sizes. A few are tall and a few are short, but most are in-between. The in-between child we call average.

Children also come in all different shapes. A few are thin, a few are fat, but most are in-between. The in-between child we call average.

In nearly everything we measure about people, we find that this is true. Anything we can measure appears from little to much with most falling in-between. These differences can be shown on a graph called the *normal curve.** It is called this because it is what we expect when we have a group of people who resemble all the people in the population.

For example, we would not expect height to fall into a normal curve if we measured all the men on a city police force. This group would contain a *bias.* That means that there is some reason why the police force is not a normal population. Because the police force will not hire men below a certain height, we would find more tall men than we would find in a normal population.

The graph of a normal population of heights of adult men might look like this. Wherever the curve is highest, there are more people who are that size. We can see from this graph that there are more men who are 5′9″ than any other height. Most men are between 5′6″ and 6 feet. Although this graph is not

_____
*The word "normal" comes from mathematics and does not necessarily mean that other curves are abnormal.

16

based on real people in a curve like this, two-thirds of the men would be between 5′6″ and 6 feet. The further you go out from the center of the curve, the fewer the number of cases. We can see that there would be very few men who are 6′6″ or 5 feet.

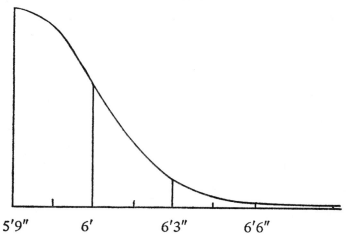

Fig. 1: Per Cent of Cases Under Portions of the Normal Curve

The graph of the police force might look like this.

5′9″   6′   6′3″   6′6″

From the graph it can be shown that police forces are biased in favor of taller men and biased against short men. This is because the police have requirements that their members not be below a certain height or above a certain height. The height of policemen is not distributed in a normal curve.

To really see whether or not measurements of people are

valid (true), we first must check out whether there are biases in what we are using to measure or biases within the group we measure. If we measure the height of people with a measuring tape that has an error of one inch, we have a biased measure. If we measure a group of people who, for some reason, have an unusually large number of short or tall people, we have a biased sample of people. If both the measuring tape and the population we measure are unbiased, we usually will find a normal curve of distributions of heights.

According to the normal curve, the position in the very middle is called the average or *mean*. That is, if we measure all the men in our population, add up the measurements and divide by the number of men measured, we can locate the middle point, the mean or what is called average. As you will probably recall from your arithmetic days, the average can be shown as follows:

	Height in Inches		
Iver	69		
Bob	66		69 or 5′9″ = Average
Matt	71	4 ⟌ 276	or Mean
Larry	70		
	276		

Generally we refer to ranges when we measure human behavior. This refers to the middle score and an equal distance on either side of the middle point which is known as the *average range*. The average range contains about two thirds of the people. Above the upper point and below the lower point of this range, is above and below the average (see Fig. 1). The lower and upper point of the average range is figured out mathematically. It involves a statistical formula called the standard deviation. A standard deviation is just what it sounds like. It is a set distance from the midpoint or average. The distance from one standard deviation below the mean to one standard deviation above the mean would include two out of three people in a normal distribution. The distance from two standard deviations below the mean to two standard deviations above the mean would include about 95 percent of people. Only one percent is outside plus three to minus three standard deviations.

The end result of all this gives us an equal number of cases on either side of the midpoint. By means of this standard deviation we can then figure out where our ranges of below or above the average are, as well as greatly below and greatly above the average.

As with our example of height, we would then be able to see at a glance, given someone's height, whether they are extremely short, somewhat short, average, above the average, or greatly above the average.

Sometimes these concepts confuse us. Particularly when they are stated in mathematical terms. However, we all use these ideas in our daily conversations. Many times we hear people say, "My, isn't he tall for his age!" Rarely do they say, "He must be about one and a half standard deviations above the mean in height for his age." But the meaning is the same.

Most of the terms, such as mean or average, standard deviation, range and normal distribution can be confusing, but need not be. Understanding in every day terms is all that is really necessary (unless, of course, you are a statistician, which obviously, we are not).

Now that we have an understanding of the normal curve, we can return to look at the infinite variations found in the family of man, and, specifically, the children in the family of man.

Children grow, develop and mature at different rates. There are average ranges for development of all kinds of skills such as speech, walking, toilet training, running, hopping, and skipping. There is no one set age at which all children will develop these skills. A few children develop all or some of these very early, a few very late, and most at an average rate. Not all who are early in developing walking are early in developing speech. There is as much difference within individual children as there is between individual children. Given good health and proper nutrition, each child will develop in his unique and individual manner. Usually this means the child will spurt, stay the same for a while, and spurt again. Not all children within the same family will have exactly the same rate of development — except, perhaps, in the case of identical twins.

We can easily see the differences, for example, between

girls and boys. In general, little girls develop in some areas, such as fine motor skills, attention span, and speech more rapidly than do little boys.

There are differences between the sexes in development which appear to have little to do with country, culture, and life style. Unfortunately, in our society, where we emphasize competition, parents often begin very early to make comparisons between their child's development and that of the neighbor's. It is as if there was something about a child's development which reflects goodness or virtue in the parent. In reality, children frequently resemble their parents, grandparents, uncles and aunts, and will develop as they are born to do — individually.

Because we are a competitive people, we often make the mistake of trying to force development. Parents become more anxious about toilet training a child when grandma is coming to visit. Some young mothers can become hurt when they meet a classmate who has a little girl with clear speech while her son is still struggling with his "r" sounds.

This form of competition can lead parents into valuing children for what they can do rather than for what they are — individuals.

Parents, as a group, love their children deeply and are concerned about their welfare. Parents sacrifice a great deal of personal freedom when they start a family. (Whenever one of us says "Where would we be without the kids?" the other always answers, "The beach in Bermuda.") In general, they are able to face the many problems of early childhood with great courage. But as they see the child leave the toddler stage and become a preschooler, their good sense often falls away, and they are racked with concern as the little child is about to enter school. No matter how hard the parents have tried to be accepting and understanding of their little one, the concern about his education and how the child will measure up to other children can cloud their basic good sense. Parents know all the horror stories about poor readiness and school failure. They can begin to view the child, not as an individual, but in terms of how he will be able to compete.

This concern is not because parents are villains. On the contrary, it stems from their deep love and concern for the child.

Sometimes it is a deeply buried memory of their own painful school experience. At other times, it is an anxiety that has been encouraged by all sorts of agencies within the society. For example, public service announcements on television and articles in the popular press sometimes suggest that an average student or, even worse, a school failure, may as well suicide at four.

It is very difficult for parents to imagine that someone in the community, such as the classroom teacher, can possibly view their child as anything other than delightful. Parents can remember the clever, kind and funny things the child has said and done. Now the child will be taking his individuality to school. Here he will be with other children, and all those little quirks which make the child so loveable at home become an area of concern. Is he ready? If not, what can I do? What is his I.Q.? (In the parents' mind, I.Q. means intelligence.) Should he go to nursery school? Have we "over-protected", "rejected", "failed to stimulate" (or whatever other current behavioral fad is available) him?

Whatever knowledge and understanding of individual differences the parents have can fall away as the child now becomes the focus of the campaign to make him acceptable to schooling.

The rest of this book will attempt to describe children in terms of their differences so that parents and teachers can make the best decision about how to make the child's life as full and happy as possible.

HOW CAN A CHILD BE SO GOOD IN ONE THING AND SO BAD IN ANOTHER?

It really does not surprise us if a good businessman is a bad bowler or if one person can drink all night while another passes out after one.

The human body is run by the brain and nervous system. Like faces, each brain is different. Even in identical twins, who shared the same cells at one time in their development, the fact that they were in different places in the womb, and that one came through the birth canal before the other, is enough to ensure that they are not exactly the same, even if they look that way.

The brain is made up of many nerve cells. These cells connect to each other and form *nerve pathways*. The brain is so complicated that we know very little about it. But is it surprising that one nerve pathway works very well and the next one over does not work as well?

But many people seem to think of the brain as if it were a fairly simple machine, like a cheap radio.

The human brain is infinitely complex. It is quite probable that everything we do involves a slightly different location on a slightly different nerve cell than something else we do which is similar. We can expect as many different talents and behaviors as there are brains. What we cannot expect is that everyone can or will develop the way adults wish.

Human beings, adults and children, rarely, if ever, show high talent in all areas of their lives. An outstanding violinist may be a poor student and an exceptionally poor athlete. The outstanding student may be very poor in relating to other people. A poor student may be an outstanding artist and sensitive to the needs of others. Rarely can a child ever fulfill the demands for perfection that are required by adults.

Many successful adults have a history of failure in childhood. What psychologist or psychiatrist in the past would have predicted that the timid, fearful little "mama's boy" who wore sunbonnets and was teased and called "skinny" by the other boys would grow up to become Robert Peary, the Arctic explorer. The little boy who did not learn his alphabet until he was nine or begin to learn to read until eleven would be considered a failure by teachers today. But, although he never learned to read well, this "problem" did not destroy President Woodrow Wilson.

Each child has his own strengths and talents and should be allowed to develop them. Today's "failing" child may be tomorrow's genius.

HOW MANY CHILDREN ARE NORMAL?

We talk so often about the "normal" child. There are two ways to talk about the idea of normal. In statistical terms, the "normal range" means from minus one to plus one standard deviation. This includes the middle two-thirds of the sample (see chart, p. 17). This is a very accurate way of thinking about normal children except it is seldom done.

What most people mean is usually a little different. To them, "normal" is the child *without* problems. How many of these should there be?

Let us say that you step out your door and there, luckily, are 100 children, 50 boys and 50 girls, all of whom are having their ninth birthday today. Let's assume that these 100 children are a perfect sample of all nine-year-olds in this country. Let us look at them in terms of what we know about children.

Twenty-five of them would have I.Q.'s of less than 90. Although many children in the I.Q. range from 90 to 110 have trouble in school, we can be pretty sure that *all* of these 25 will have problems with academic learning. Seventy-five normal children left.

Many experts in reading like to call the lowest 20 percent in reading as reading problems. Since we know that reading problems exist in all I.Q. ranges, we can guess that 15 of our 75 children will have problems in reading which will interfere with their school work. Sixty left.

Two of these children will be super students; that is, they are so good in school learning that nothing that goes on in the classroom turns them on. One child may be physically handicapped. Fifty-seven left. When teachers are asked how many of their children have "emotional" problems that interfere with their behavior, they have been known to answer as much as 70 percent. But most teachers say about 30 percent. Thus, 17 of our 57 may have behavior problems which will get them in trouble. That leaves 40 of our 100 who are left as "normal".

We have played with numbers here. There is a good chance that many of our reading problems would also be counted as behavior problems, so we may have counted them twice. On the other hand, we did not count many other problems described in this book which may have further reduced our number.

Thus, it looks like more than half of all children could be seen as abnormal. It can get worse. One study in New York felt that 85 percent of adults had mental problems. If more than half are abnormal, this means it is normal from the statistical point of view.

We must conclude that the normal human condition is to be abnormal.

I.Q.

The *Intelligence Quotient*, or I.Q., is a score on a test. It is a rather recent concept, although testing humans with measuring instruments is not new. For example, in 1115 B.C., the Chinese developed examinations for people applying for government jobs. These were not much different from the tests given today; in fact, in some ways they were better. Their tests were "job samples," which is what we try to make our tests like today. The idea is that whatever behavior is needed for a job can be sampled in small doses and give you an idea of how people will do on the job itself.

Around the turn of the twentieth century, Alfred Binet, a French psychologist, began a series of studies on differences between children who were good in school and those who were not. In 1904, he was asked by the officials of the Paris schools to identify children who would fail in school.

In 1905, Binet and Simon published their first "intelligence" scale. Several revisions later, they produced a test in 1911 which is pretty much like the tests we use today.

In 1916, an American version of the test was built and the Stanford-Binet is probably the most commonly used individually administered I.Q. test around. It used to give scores in terms of "Mental Age", but this concept was so misleading that only the I.Q. score is given today.

In 1939, the first edition of the Wechsler scales was published. There are several Wechsler tests in use now, all of them giving a Verbal I.Q., a Performance I.Q., and a Full Scale I.Q.

The items used on the tests were chosen so that children who did well in school would do well on these items, average students would do just so-so, and poor students would have difficulties with the items on the test.

Thus, such tests are to give us a *prediction* on how the child *should* do in school. They are given to only one child at a time and a trained psychologist must give the test. There is almost no reading on the tests.

Both the Binet and Wechsler scales give *standard scores*. Standard scores are scores based on the normal curve described on pp. 16-19. In other words, children's scores are fitted into the normal distribution so that we know how many children should get any one I.Q. score. It can be seen from the following figure that an I.Q. of 100 is average; that is, 50 percent of the children should score above 100 and 50 percent should score below. The two tests differ slightly in terms of their distributions. On the Stanford-Binet the 68 percent of children who are in *the average range* score between 84 and 116, while the same children should score between 85 and 115 on the Wechsler tests. It is the Wechsler I.Q.'s which are indicated on the accompanying figure.

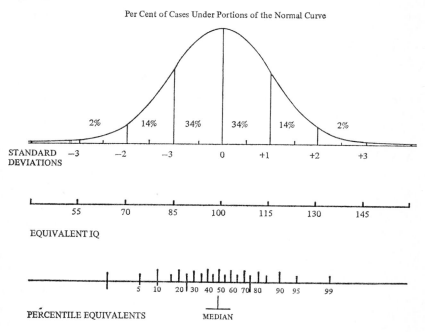

Per Cent of Cases Under Portions of the Normal Curve

I.Q. scores are fairly consistent. If a child is given two tests at two different times, we expect a difference of as much as 6 or 8 points between the two tests and change of 20 points are quite rare, but not unknown. There can be many reasons for such large changes. The day the test was given, the conditions under which it was given, the physical health of the child, the amount of anxiety shown by the child, and how the psychologist and child got along all can have some minor and temporary effects on the score.

Besides, it is really not the score that is important, but how the child gets the score. On the Stanford-Binet, all types of test items are mixed into the I.Q. score. On the Wechsler tests, there are six "Verbal" tests and five "Performance" tests which are usually given. Each test gives its own score (which is also a standard score) and the Verbal and Performance I.Q.'s are computed. In the hands of a competent psychologist, what happens during the test is much more important than the score.

Both tests are heavily weighted with verbal tasks. In almost all cases, even Performance tests, the child is asked a question or told what to do. Since the test is supposed to tell how a child does in school, this is probably appropriate because school is so heavily weighted with verbal tasks.

I.Q. tests involve having the child say something or do something. They may have to define a word ("What is a cup?"), draw something ("Draw a square for me here"), remember something ("Say 4-6-3-2"), see relationships ("Which is bigger?" or "How are a fish and a whale alike?"), give a socially correct answer ("Why shouldn't you steal?"), figure out how to put things together ("Put these pieces together so they look like a dog."), think arithmetically ("How many cars are 2 cars and 3 cars?"), have profited from exposure to the American culture ("When is Lincoln's birthday?"), see relationships in pictures ("What is missing here?"), recognize vocabulary ("which picture is an airplane?"), and such other tasks.*

Some schools of psychology still teach their students to read more into the scores on these types of questions than they should. For example, the test of remembering a series of numbers is thought by some to measure anxiety. There is no evidence that we can read anything more into a score than what we can see. In the same example, a child who does poorly on remembering numbers can only be said to be having trouble in remembering numbers. He may be able to remember words well. However, if the child confuses "13" and "30," we should look to see if he is having auditory discrimination problems (see pp. 50-51).

There are other tests which are called I.Q. tests. These break down into two major groups:

---

*The examples given are, for the most part, not actual questions, but are very similar to actual questions or tasks given on the Wechsler or Binet tests.

A. *Individual Tests* — There have been many attempts to find shorter I.Q. tests which take less than the forty-five minutes to an hour it takes to give a Stanford-Binet or Wechsler. One type are tests which give fewer items than the longer I.Q. tests but resemble them remarkably. These are usually used for screening children only, to see who should be given a longer examination. Another type gives only one kind of task, such as vocabulary, matching pictures, etc. They take almost no time to give, but are not very useful, ordinarily.

B. *Group Tests* — Most children receive tests in school which are called I.Q. tests. Paper and pencil are used and the children take them in groups.

Calling such tests I.Q. tests confuses things. Unlike the other tests, they require reading, and usually working with a pencil and paper, with no chance for the child to show individually what he can or cannot do.

On the other hand, such tests are so much like most school tasks that in some ways they are probably more accurate in measuring school-type ability. But they give little or no information that is not picked up on an achievement test.

The I.Q.'s of parents and children are quite similar. There is very little question about this. Minority groups get very angry about people saying this because it is interpreted as if blacks, native Americans, and others *inherit* a lesser "intelligence" than whites, who have a higher average I.Q. than do most minority groups. There are obviously differences between groups, even among the whites. Some ethnic groups usually score high and some score low.*

The terrible thing about the whole testing system is, first, the arrogance of the whites to assume that what *they* do well is intelligent behavior and, second, the fact that many black and Mexican-American leaders have bought the intelligence argument. These black and Mexican-American leaders want to throw

---

*There is a great deal of similarity in how whites and non-whites of the *same* social class perform on I.Q. tests. Non-whites cannot truly be compared with whites because their culture is different and they are certainly poorer and getting more so all the time. Minority leaders claim, and rightly so, that the tests reflect only the white culture. Can you imagine that an Indian would lose a point on one test if he did not answer "Columbus" or "the Vikings" to the question of who discovered America?

out I.Q. tests because black and Spanish speaking children do
poorly on them. This is like the old kings who chopped off the
head of the messenger who brought bad news. The thing to remember is that the test only reflects the school curriculum. If the
curriculum was changed tomorrow so that it was relevant to both
whites and non-whites, major publishing houses would have new
tests out in a year to correspond with this new curriculum. On
these new tests, white and non-whites would probably do equally
well.

The tests are excellent. They do what they are supposed to
do, The thing to question is not whether the I.Q. tests are intelligent tests, but whether the school curriculum is reasonable.

WHAT IS THE DIFFERENCE BETWEEN I.Q. AND INTELLIGENCE?

You will notice that, wherever possible, we left the word
"intelligence" out of our discussion of I.Q. Unfortunately, many
people seem to think that a test that has the word "intelligence"
in the title must measure how smart you are. Also, most people
use the word "intelligent" to describe how much schooling a
person has had.

This is due, in part, to the fact that the first "intelligence"
tests were used to measure how well a child did in school. And
I.Q. (or intelligence) tests *do* measure how well a child does in
school. In fact, these tests are probably the best ones invented
in terms of a test predicting human behavior. But they only
predict one kind of behavior, and that is school learning.

The important thing to ask is, is school learning the only
kind of intelligence? It must be remembered that I.Q. tests were
designed to predict who will do well in school and who will not.
The tests were built by looking at the children in school to see
who did well and who did not. But when these tests were first
built, mainly only rich people went to school beyond the first few
years. For example, *no* black children were included in either
Binet's original Paris sample or Wechsler's American sample.

Societies in Europe and North America have one idea of
what intelligence is. This may be very different from what the
Chinese, Eskimos, American Indians, and Kenyans think is intelligent behavior. And who is to say who is right? Piaget, the

famous Swiss psychologist, defines intelligence as the development of a logical mind that can make use of experiences. Therefore, there must be *all kinds* of intelligences. The child who lives in the north must learn how to survive in the woods, by intelligently learning what different things mean and how best to use them. The poor slum child must learn survival skills — how to exist on the street without getting hurt, while taking advantage of what is available in order to survive. School-smart children may or may not be able to do such things. Many behaviors are very independent of how children learn in school.

Certainly, school learning *can't* be the only kind of intelligence around. For example, there is research on salesmen. It may take a college degree to *get* some jobs in sales. But in those jobs that both college and high school graduates can get, we usually find that there is no relationship between the amount of schooling and success as a salesman. In other words, some of the good salesmen are found among college graduates, while as many high school graduates do well in sales. Most successful managers in business did not do well in college, but wind up hiring and firing Ph.D.'s.

School learning is a special kind of thinking, as are all kinds of learning. We find that the intelligent car mechanics around a college campus fix the cars for professors who have a different kind of intelligence. When the professor's car breaks down, the car mechanic's intelligence is more important.

This is probably why poorer students in school often become interested in cars. After years of failing in school, where langauge is so important, he can find success in dealing with things. But think of the waste! Why only cars? There are thousands of job titles that require an interest and an ability in working with things. We met one young man who was almost unintelligible when it came to communicating verbally, but was an absolute whiz when it came to wiring a computer. A president of an engineering company once told that none of his engineers were very literate, but they sure understood drawings.

It is very important to stress to a child that he *can* act intelligently. Just about *every* child can do something well. His parents and teachers should stress to him that, in those areas, he *is* acting intelligently. But he should also be told that everyone is different, that everyone has their own strengths and weaknesses, and that trying to compare himself to others is a fool's game, because everybody is different.

Certainly, if I.Q. means intelligence, we should pass laws to assure that all persons, when filing for elected positions to govern our country, take an I.Q. test and score over 100. Unfortunately, this might seriously deplete the number of candidates in the executive, legislative, *and* judicial arms of our government.

WHAT IS GENIUS AND MENTAL RETARDATION?

Scores on I.Q. tests are put into categories like this:

I.Q. of below 50	— trainable mental retardation
I.Q. of 50 to 75	— educable mental retardation
I.Q. of 75 to 90	— dull normal
I.Q. of 90 to 110	— average
I.Q. of 110 to 125	— bright normal
I.Q. of 125 to 140	— superior
I.Q. of 141 and above	— genius

These categories can vary. For example, the most important study of "genius" used youngsters in the 130's and higher on I.Q. tests. In some states, mental retardation is set at an I.Q. of 75 or below, in other states they may go up to 80 or down to 70.

On pages 24-25, it was seen that there is a certain percentage of children who fall in each of these ranges. These percentages are set by the normal curve. In other words, all that mental retardation means is that a child scores in about the lowest five percent of children on I.Q. tests. Genius means they score in the top one or two percent.

There are two kinds of retarded children. Most (about 85%) retarded children are the children of retarded or nearly retarded parents. However, some people get called "retarded" because they cannot take the tests which are given in English. People who speak Spanish cannot take tests in English and, thus, look retarded. Nevertheless, there is no question that such people are in the lowest five percent on language-based tests. It is the word "retarded" which is misleading, since many such people do quite well in surviving in the world.

Others, whose parents are usually more middle classed, get

that way from a physical problem, such as brain injury. This second group usually have the greatest difficulty and are usually more retarded than the others.

Educationally, retarded children are divided into two groups. *Educable mentally retarded* children can be placed in special classes where basically they get academic instruction (reading, arithmetic, etc.) but at a slower pace. Sometimes, when looking at professional journals aimed at teachers of the E.M.R. or E.M.H. child (educable mentally retarded or handicapped) we get the feeling that academics is *all* people figure they should be taught.

Trainable retarded children should be taught in their special classes how to care for themselves. Personal hygiene, dressing, communication skills should be emphasized. Because reading is so overvalued, some centers even emphasize teaching it to trainable children who may not even know how to dress themselves well.

Research shows that many children who score poorly on I.Q. tests do very well in living. For example, poor children may learn at a very young age how to survive on the streets but do poorly in school. Some higher scorers on I.Q. tests may need more protection until they learn what the world is all about.

Genius is even more difficult to describe. Thomas Edison's mother pulled him out of school at a very young age and he never went back. He was viewed by his teachers as dull witted. One of the "geniuses" of mass production once sued someone for libel because this person had said that this automotive marvel had the ability of a fourth grader. The "genius" lost the suit.

Thus school genius and retardation only tell how a child does in school. Even here, how well the child conforms has something to do with it. One of us once worked in a school district of 10,000 children. Since five percent of them *should* have been mentally retarded, 500 of them should have been in special classes for the mentally retarded. In truth, only 45 of them were. Somewhere were about 450 kids whose I.Q.'s were below 75, but nobody noticed them because they did not cause trouble.

As for genius, most of the people tried at Nuremberg for war crimes in World War II had I.Q.'s in the so-called "genius" range. Genius does not necessarily mean that their genius is being used for niceness instead of evil.

The chances are that many of you know someone who has an I.Q. in either the retarded or genius range. But since no one told you that, and these people are no longer in school, you do not recognize them as retardates or geniuses. One can graduate from that official category just by graduating from school. Then, once out of school, it is performance that counts.

This performance is demonstrated by doing something creative. Examining the lives of creative people in history, we find that many did poorly in school. Many of them would score quite low on an I.Q. test. Once we look at a person's performance over his life-time, the "genius" status in school is very unimportant. A true "genius" is someone who is creative and unusual, and contributes to society in an original manner. Schooling is independent of genius. The Goertzels, in *Cradles of Eminence*, tell us that Zola failed in literature, that Eugene O'Neill, Faulkner, and F. Scott Fitzgerald failed in college. Gamal Nasser failed both second and third grades. Einstein and Edison were considered dull in school. Sister Kenny had only six years of schooling. These are extreme cases. But many people could achieve — at a lesser level — given the chance.

COMPETITION

Our society is becoming so competitive that sometimes we think that soon no one will be able to succeed. As we are attempting to show in this book, almost all the ways we have to rate children involve comparing them to each other. And we are beginning to rate them in everything, from how fast they begin to talk to how early they achieve each educational milestone.

In the early grades, teachers put up a star chart. Youngsters who have talent for reading and writing get stars, while the others do not. By second or third grade, every kid knows who will get the most stars. Even the value of the stars as rewards soon drops when all but the good students realize that they are out of the running from the start.

But the awful part is that these children are usually competing in things that they have no more control over than they do their height. The olympic reader has it made in the school, just as the olympic athlete has it made on the field. However, it is even less fair in the reading competition than in the sports competition. To compete in sports, the child has to have both talent and an aggressive desire to beat the next guy. If a child has athletic talent but does not have the need to win, he will probably never fulfill his potential on the field of play. To some extent, children can choose *not* to compete in games. In school they have no choice.

We feel that competition in schools — for grades, for the teachers' approval, and for their parent's approval — should be cut down.

Some parents have figured out that if they hold up one brother or sister as an example to another, they may set up a situation in the home where the kids are always fighting. How can you like someone who is portrayed as either superior or inferior to you?

Each child is an individual in his own right. He should be appreciated as such. If we could set up a society where, instead of constantly pitting one child against another, children could cooperate with each other more, balancing off one child's weakness with another's strength, it might be a happier world.

ACHIEVEMENT TESTING

The history of achievement testing is interesting because it shows how easily things can go haywire. In his popular text, *Essentials of Psychological Testing*, Dr. Lee Cronbach summarizes their history:

> The first systematic comparison of school attainment was made by an educational crusader, J. M. Rice, in 1897. Rice was convinced that the pressure for perfection in certain types of achievement was leading to faulty emphasis in education, and prepared a test of spelling ability to determine what results could be expected. His test was given in twenty-one scattered cities and showed that, regardless of the time devoted to spelling, the test scores of eighth-graders were about the same in all cities. He showed further that although children in some cities were superior in spelling during early grades, presumably because of stress on that subject, such differences vanished by the end of schooling. It is ironical that Rice hoped by such evidence to show that the time spent on formal learning could be re-

duced, saving more time for an enriched curriculum. Instead, the
testing movement which he fathered became a factor tending to
hold the schools to limited curricula.

Educators were quickly impressed with the advantages of de-
termining when schools were "up to standard," and tests of reading
and arithmetic were prepared and widely used. Tests in other subjects followed rapidly.

Dr. Cronbach later states,

. . . the very powers sought in standardized testing have been a
two-edged weapon, damaging the educational program as much as
helping it. The essential difficulty is that *achievement tests determine the curriculum.* Both college students and younger pupils
devote much of their time trying to determine what will be tested,
so that they can study that material and neglect anything else. . . .
The teacher too is driven by the test to direct his energies into the
paths they dictate.

Achievement test scores can be valuable, but only if used
correctly. Unfortunately, most teachers and parents do not have
the technical background to use them properly. Achievement
tests should be used for research purposes, and to help in administrative decisions in the school.

If the teacher uses them to help a youngster, they can also
be useful. For example, if such a test shows that a youngster is
doing well in science, the teacher might use scientific experiments
to teach the child other things. However, some schools are dropping these tests because people are unhappy about giving them
and taking them. But rather than examining how these test scores
could be used to learn about students as individuals, or how the
scores can be used to evaluate the academic impact of a learning
program, some schools have just quit gathering the information.
Often, having testing programs is like owning a computer. They
are very nice but you have to understand their language.

We feel that the misuse of testing programs can be blamed
almost totally on the competitiveness of the society, and on the
pressures on teachers to conform and succeed where "success"
is not possible. Once, one of us was doing a research project
using these tests to see if a program was successful. We kept
telling the teachers that we would not analyze the scores by
class, or even by school. Despite this, many angry phone calls

came from teachers who felt they hadn't enough time to prepare for the test. One teacher even went out and got his own copy of the test to teach parts of it to his students (see section on teacher accountability, pp. 81-82).

Many schools send home scores on achievement tests. Little does the parent know what the tests measure, what the scores mean, or how much of a difference between scores is significant.

Commonly used achievement tests include the Iowa Tests and the Stanford Achievement Tests. Most achievement tests give about ten different scores. Most achievement tests also give a composite score, which is an average of the different subtest scores. This single score is usually given in a grade equivalent or in a percentile. Problems in understanding these terms are described in the section on Reading Tests (pp. 37-42), which are a special kind of achievement test.

Most achievement tests are given in a group situation. Almost the whole test involves reading. This makes them very hard for children who do not read well.

Achievement tests can be useful in that they give some idea of how well the child is learning the things that are important on the achievement test without considering other things. For example, we have seen many children who score well on achievement tests but do poorly in teacher ratings. These are obviously problems in either the child's behavior or in the teacher's personality. Having an achievement test score available on a child like this allows you to get the *real* problem out in the open.

Tests should be a tool. Like all tools, people should learn *how* to use them before using them. And like other tools, if you use them wrongly, they are useless.

HOW DO WE TEST READING?

Many discussions between parents and teachers deal with the level at which the child is reading. There are basically two ways to measure reading:

1) *Reading Tests* — There are two types of reading tests:
   a) *Group Tests* — These usually have the children read passages and then answer questions about each passage. They have a limited time to do them. What is

basically measured in group reading tests is how fast the child can read, and how well he understands what he reads. Thus, the child who does best on these tests is the one who can skim well, whose language is so well developed that the words will be easy for him, or who is so good at test-taking that he would answer the questions well whether he read the stuff or not. The child who has to read word-by-word or has a tough time figuring out what the words mean will do poorly. Scores are usually reported in *percentiles,* which tell what percent of children yours beats out.

b) *Individual Tests* — These are usually given by a psychologist or some other educational specialist. The child reads either words or passages aloud. Sometimes he is asked questions aloud and must answer these. Basically, we are measuring *word recognition,* since we assume that a child must properly call the word before he understands it. Scores are usually given in terms of grade equivalents. For example, a child who scores at the 4.5 grade level is reading at the 5th month (of a 10 month school year) of the 4th grade level.

2) *Informal evaluations* are usually of two types. The classroom teacher will talk of a child who is reading in a 4-1 text book. This means that the child is currently reading in the text book which is deemed appropriate for the "average" child in the first half of the 4th grade.

An *Informal reading inventory* is usually done by a reading specialist. The child is given a group of passages of text which coincide with what is thought appropriate for children who are doing average work. The child reads these passages aloud. The highest passage he reads with mistakes on fewer than ten or fifteen percent of the words is seen as his "functional reading level." In this case, the reading specialist will also ask questions to see how well he understands what was read.

The most important part of any evaluation are the clues that the tester gets in terms of how to teach the child.

WHAT IS BEING MEASURED BY READING TESTS?

Many reading tests have different scores for the different things that go to make up reading. For example, a test may have one score for how well a child can blend two sounds, like "s" and "p" into "sp", another score for whether he properly hears the differences in similar sounding words like "dog" and "hog", a score for whether he uses punctuation correctly, etc.

But basically, reading involves measuring three broad areas:

1) *Word recognition* is the basic requirement of reading. In order to use a printed word, the child must be able to know the meanings of a group of letters (like d-o-g must mean something more to the child than the three letters in the word). Another way children figure out words is to guess the meaning of the word from the words around it. For example, in the sentence, "The _____ ate the bone", the reader may not have to know how to actually read the word that goes in the blank. He can guess it without even having to figure out what the word actually says.

Children with severe difficulties in word recognition are sometimes called *dyslexics*. However, there is very little agreement between professionals as to how to define or diagnose dyslexia. Basically, it suggests a child with a normal verbal I.Q. (who can handle spoken language adequately), but who cannot recognize words as easily as teachers expect him to.

2) *Efficiency* in reading means the *speed* at which a child can read and understand. For example, a child may actually recognize the words in a passage, but it may be so difficult for him to figure out each word separately, that he gets nothing out of the passage. On the other hand, some children can skim quite well but also miss the details of what was written. Some individually administered tests do not measure speed or, if they do, it is the speed of *oral* reading which may be quite different from how fast a child can read silently. In fact, for years reading experts have wondered if reading aloud required any thinking at all about what was being read. On group tests, speed is usually measured by seeing how fast a child can read a passage silently. But then we do not know whether it was read or skimmed, so we

usually ask him about the passage to see if he understood it. This leads us to the most difficult thing to measure.

3) *Comprehension* measures whether a child understands what he is reading. Among professionals in the field of reading, arguments still rage on how to measure this. We feel that, in most cases, if a child can accurately and efficiently recognize a written word, he can understand it as well or as poorly as he can understand the same word if he hears it correctly. In other words, we feel that the comprehension of written language should be no different than the comprehension of spoken language, all other things being equal.

Certainly, the child who is having a hard time figuring out what a written word is, but eventually gets it, may have a lot of trouble putting a group of such words together into a meaningfull thought. Had he heard that sentence, he would have understood it better. However, that child's problem is in word recognition more than in comprehension.

For this reason, we feel that a child's reading comprehension is best improved by making him more efficient in word recognition. The closer his ability to recognize a written word is to his ability to hear that word, the better. Any other interpretation of how to train reading comprehension suggests that, through training, we can get a child to the point where he can comprehend a written word *better* than he could understand that word if he heard it right. It is very doubtful that this can be done in children.

Another example of the problem of using comprehension as a measure of reading is found in children we call hyperlexics. *Hyperlexics* are children who are able to recognize printed words quite easily and efficiently, and yet are unable to comprehend them. This situation would be like that in which some people find themselves when reading a foreign language which they had studied at one time. They often find that they are able to orally read the language quite fluently and efficiently even though their comprehension is quite limited because of the word-by-word translation required. Hyperlexics also recognize words well above their expected levels, and yet do not comprehend them better than their verbal skills would allow. It would be reasonable to suggest that a child whose verbal skills are low would be unable to comprehend language with the ability of a child with verbal skills in the superior range, even though both children were able to recognize printed words with equal quickness and accuracy.

Because teachers and parents often use a child's reading level to estimate how "smart" the child is, the hyperlexic child can have a lot of trouble. We have seen cases of real problems because a child could recognize words better than he could understand them. For example, one boy was skipped ahead when in second grade because he could word recognize (call the words right) on the fifth grade level. When he did get to fifth grade he was having trouble because his teacher expected super work from him and he could not produce. In second grade, most of what is taught is word recognition. By fifth grade, you have to *use* your reading in order to figure things out. This child could read (word recognize) well, he just could not figure things out as well as everybody expected of him.

It is important to understand that there is very little relationship between the score on a child's reading test and his score on an I.Q. test. Let us say we take a group of children in a narrow range of I.Q.'s, like selecting all the children in your town's fourth grade who have I.Q.'s between 100 and 110. In that group we will find almost as many children reading below grade level as are reading above grade level. If we then take all the children with I.Q.'s between 90 and 100, we will find almost as many reading above grade level as are reading below.*

We cannot use a child's reading level to judge him as "intelligent" or not. Reading is just one of the many skills that make up a child.

---

*Reading and I.Q. are correlated. This means that if you take a large group of children, those with higher I.Q.'s will probably read at a higher level than low I.Q. children. But in terms of individual children, the correlation is not high enough to be useful. Some children with high I.Q.'s will not read as well as other children with low I.Q.'s, while some other children with high I.Q.'s will read much better than the average and below children. In fact, when we look at children within a narrow range of I.Q.'s, like all children in the 100 to 110 range, we find pretty much a normal distribution of reading scores in that group, with some high, more average, and some low.

WHAT DOES A READING SCORE MEAN?

We mentioned above a child who was reading at the 4.5 grade level. What does this mean? It means that the test authors selected a series of material to include in the test, and then administered these materials to a group representing the population for whom the test was intended (in this case, fourth grade children). And let us say that the intention of the test was that it be given half way through 4th grade. Materials would be selected for the test and the test score exceeded by 50 percent of this group is then equated to grade level. Therefore, the 4.5 grade level simply means that 50 percent of the children at that grade level were able to read at that score or better, while 50 percent read below that point.

The rest of the scores are set into a normal curve (see pp. 16-19). Although too complicated to go into here, most reading tests are built so that there is a five grade spread in any one grade. In other words, the tests are *built* so that children in grade 4.5 should score between grade 2.0 and grade 7.0. About two-thirds of children will be reading between grade 3.5 and grade 5.5 level.

Measured reading is a relative — not an absolute — concept. In clinical practice or in schools, one seldom, if ever, sees a child beyond the first or second grade level who is totally unable to read, unless there is frank brain trauma. Totally illiterate children have almost totally disappeared except among minority groups that are excluded from education. One sees, rather, efficient, average, or inefficient readers, and then only insofar as our narrowly set limits for expected behavior permits.

To repeat, by definition, 50 percent of the children *must* read below grade level. If we were to invent "instant learning" and this resulted in each child increasing one grade level in reading, what would be the outcome? The only thing that would happen would be that a child who is reading in a fourth grade textbook today would be reading in a fifth grade textbook tomorrow. We would then change the name of the fifth grade textbook to "fourth grade textbook," and 50 percent of the children in fourth grade would still be below that point. The child who yesterday was reading at the third grade level and after the "instant learning" moved up to the fourth grade level would still find himself in the bottom reading group in his class. In other words, there is *no* such thing as an absolute level of reading at which we can expect people to perform. Changes over time, the population becoming educated, new textual materials, improvements in communications technology, and the like, all affect the relative difficulty of materials which we call "fourth grade reading." Today's fourth grade reading materials may be the third or fifth grade level of twenty years ago or twenty years from now, depending upon these and other factors.

These kinds of scores, whether they be in grade level terms or percentiles (the 60th percentile is the score on the test where 60 percent of the children tested scored below) are developed by using a *norm group*. The norm group is the group of children who were first tested and, using their scores, the scores for each grade equivalent or percentile are obtained. Test makers try to get a sample of children from all over the country, rich and poor, white and non-white, to use for their norm group.

But what happens? Many school districts develop *local norms*. What they do is take the scores obtained by the children in *their* school district and norm the test on them, rather than on the test-maker's national norm group. Thus, it is conceivable that in an area such as Minnesota, where the average I.Q. is higher than most of the rest of the country, 60 to 70 percent of the children in a school district may be reading above their grade level when grade level is figured on a national norm group. Nevertheless, 50 percent of the children in the school district are still reading below "average," when average is established on their fellow students in their own school district. An interesting outcome of this situation was that an inner-city school, involved in one of our projects, is typically a focus of new remedial reading methods because of the low reading level. However, the average reading level in that school was based on local norms; and, according to national norms, the students in this sample *were* at about their grade level in achievement. Since we have made such a national fetish of "reading at grade level," communicating this interpretation to the teachers seemed to improve their morale.

One other problem has to do with *which* test you use. We

gave one group of 100 third grade children four different reading tests that had word recognition scores. All tests were given at about the same time and all are often used in schools.

The group scored a full grade *higher* on one test than one of the others. The other two tests fell about half way in between.

If a teacher wants to look good, she should give the low scoring test at the beginning of the year and the high scoring test at the end of the year. That way, her group will look like it really learned, whether it did or not.

This points out the dangers of using tests to rate children. There really is no need to use tests this way. Tests should be used to help children — to see what their strengths and weaknesses are, and to give the teacher an idea of *how* to teach them or what to teach them.

Unfortunately, many tests are used to show that one child is better than another, one school is better than another, or one school district is better than another. This is a misuse of tests and does the children and the teachers no good. It forces teachers into teaching the children the materials on the test which will be used to rate them. In this way, we can artificially raise the scores on tests. This is why so many expensive testing programs are useless.

READABILITY

A typical letter to a parent from a school might begin, "In order to expedite the movement of children between classes, the administration and teaching staff of our school have recently concluded a series of planning studies dealing with traffic patterns." Compare this to saying it in another way: "We have been trying to move children from class to class more easily. Our staff has just finished a series of meetings on this."

All too often, one of the greatest problems in written communication between teachers and children, parents, or other teachers is the fact that it is so difficult for some people to write at a low level of difficulty. The level of difficulty of a group of sentences is called the *readability* level. There are formulas for readability, and it is said that at least one popular magazine uses these formulas to make sure its articles can be read more easily than are most other magazines.

Readability can be a problem in many areas, as suggested on pp. 43-44. It is, therefore, very important to keep this in mind when writing. There are a few simple rules which can be followed:

1. Use 2 or 3 short, easy words instead of 1 long, hard one.
2. Keep sentences short.
3. Make it personal — whenever possible, talk of "we feel" or "I said," instead of "it has been stated."
4. Keep in mind that reading is hard for many people.

Readability is very important in the classroom as well. As a general rule, text authors aim their readability level for grade level, thus making the reading difficult for 50 percent of the students. However, a recent study of 23 intermediate grade (4-6) texts in Indiana found that none of the texts examined appeared to be written in such a way as to be at a more difficult level of readability at the end of the text than they were at the beginning. Within each text, there was a wide range of levels of readability, thus assuring that even the good reader will have difficulty with some passages.

One would think that, given the huge sums paid for textbooks in this country, more attention would be paid to whether the audience at which these books are aimed can read them. Since most of the knowledge children are supposed to get in school comes from textbooks, it must be recognized that this is a very inefficient means of learning for probably more than half of the students.

HOW MANY PEOPLE READ WHEN THEY GET OUT OF SCHOOL?

In a recent Gallup Poll, 58 percent of the adults polled admitted that they have *never* read a book from cover to cover. Most people read only when necessary. Newspaper studies show that people seldom read more than headlines and a few simple features.

In a recent poll done by Louis Harris, they gave people a sample of basic application forms for such things as getting a

Social Security card, a driver's license, or a bank loan. They developed a "literacy survival index" and estimated that almost 19 million Americans cannot read well enough to deal with many of these forms.

This is because reading is difficult for most people. People *learn* in all kinds of ways, including television, talking to others, movies, watching others, radio, and by doing. But despite the fact that our society feels that most good knowledge is in books, very few people read them. And the world goes on.

PROBLEMS IN HANDWRITING

In order to use a pencil, whether to write or print, a child must have some ability to control the muscles he will need for this. Writing requires some very small movements in order to get a series of lines in the right place. Like any other physical activity, whether it is dancing or ping-pong, some people can do it easily while it is hard for others.

Watch children when they are first learning to use a pencil. Their little fingers are wrapped tight around the pencil, so tight that the ends of the fingers often turn white from the effort.

As they grow, these muscles become well coordinated in some children. But for some children, the effort is always painful because it is so hard for them. Their fingers hurt.

Sometimes teachers or parents do not realize this. Long written assignments can cause physical pain in those youngsters whose finger coordination skills are not mature enough to handle them.

We saw one girl who was in fourth grade. She had exceptional talent for school and could read like a whiz. She was one of those few children who found school very easy and was learning very well. But she was flunking.

Her school insisted that she do long assignments in her workbook. Not only were these tasks boring to her, but long written tasks pained her fingers. Finally, she rebelled and would not do her workbook. Since she had little to do, she acted up a little out of boredom. The school got angry.

We tried to point out that she was learning well, that she could not do long writing tasks, and what was so great about workbook assignments anyway? The school principal was much less interested in how much she learned — they wanted her to *obey*. We tried to point out that workbooks were a cop-out, that teachers used them to keep children busy while they did other things and that it would probably be just as well (in many cases) if the kids sat around and daydreamed. The school refused to budge.

Every year we got in touch with the new teacher and asked that this girl's writing assignments be kept very short. We also suggested that they rate her on her performance in the classroom, instead of group tests that are machine scored.*

Each year the school insisted on the holiness of writing instead of trying a humane approach.

This girl's behavior got worse and worse as she and the school stayed at war over the workbook. Finally, after a couple of years, the school gave in out of desperation. When we last heard, she was at the top of her class in terms of what she was doing in the classroom and everyone was happy.

Watch a child's fingers when he writes. Is it hard for him? Does he have trouble staying on the line? Do lines which should be straight get curvy because he can't control his fingers? Does he start off fast and slow right down to a crawl? Is the writing on the first line legible and becomes illegible lower down? Does he try to avoid doing the writing, when avoiding it is more trouble than doing it?

If the answer to any of these is yes, cut down the amount of writing required. See if teaching him to type works better. Let him show what he knows by telling it or dictating it into a machine. How many businessmen ever write? They dictate it and it gets typed. Most people write very little. Give the kids a break too.

---

*Machine scored tests involve making tiny little marks between little lines or in little circles. Many children lose their place easily on such tests, or they get so tired making these little marks with their pencil that they eventually can't make them in between the little lines. If they miss exactly the right spot, the answer comes out wrong on the scoring machine. If a teacher is forced to use such tests, they should always skim the answer sheet for near misses and count them right.

WHAT IF A CHILD IS LEFT-HANDED?

In the old days, some people found that poor readers seem to be found more among left-handers than right-handers. Using some extremely poor logic, they decided to try to switch left-handers to being right-handed. Sometimes we wonder whether, if some researcher finds that fat people are good readers, parents and teachers will begin to stuff their children with food.

Now we know more about handedness. We find some people are very right-handed, some do a little more with their right than left, some use both hands equally, some are a little more left than right-handed, and some are left-handed in everything. Add to this the fact that some people are left-eyed and some right-eyed, and some are left-footed and some right-footed.

In other words, if we were able to precisely measure handedness, we might find that it came out something like the normal curve described in Chapter III but probably somewhat overrepresented on the right-handers' side.

Some left-handers become very good readers. Leave the child alone and let him select which hand he wants to use. By the age of 10 or 12, he will have decided (if he ever is going to decide). There is no need to discuss it at all, except to warn the child about certain problems. Much of the world acts like there are no such things as left-handers. It is hard to find desks, scissors, brushes, etc., for left-handers. But don't ever place a value judgment on which hand a child uses.

NEW VERSUS OLD MATH

We would love to have a nickel for every parent who has complained to us about their troubles in helping their children with their math homework. The problem is that the parents do not understand how to do it. And, usually, neither do their kids.

Traditional math is what most of us remember. First we learned how to add and subtract, then we learned how to multiply and divide. During this period we also learned our tables. We all remember struggling with our "eight times" table until we could recite it like our own name. Then, when we got to secondary school, we learned algebra, geometry, and other pretty distinct bodies of mathematical knowledge.

However, some people were not satisfied with the results of this learning. When it came to *applying* math, many kids were having trouble. In the mad days following the Soviet launching of Sputnik, American education became a great big funnel. Into the top went all of our students with their different talents and interests, and out of the bottom was supposed to come engineers and "hard" scientists. The mathematical theory necessary to deal with computer programming, statistics, and physics had to be taught at the college or post-graduate level.

Mathematicians have some of the same problems that the rest of us do. Like most of the rest of us, they reasoned that what was good for them must be good for everybody. Thus, we got new math with its aim to teach children the theory of mathematics rather than the old way, with its emphasis on rote memory. The idea is that, if you know the idea behind solving problems, you can figure out how to solve the problem.

This is correct, but it is only correct for those people who can figure out the idea behind the problem. Evidently many children cannot figure this out well. Achievement tests, which were built using old math, showed a drop in math scores as more and more schools began using new math. The children were supposedly learning how to solve problems, but were not doing a very good job in solving the old math problems.

New math is very good to have if you are going on to advanced algebra. It is a lot more fun to learn if you have math talent. It allows you to deal with the ideas needed for calculus, experimental design, or computer programming. But if you do not have the type of math talent that will allow you to finally wind up in advanced algebra, new math will kill you. It requires too much aptitude, abstraction, and attention for the average or below average student. By trying to force them to look like everybody else, we are not only putting them through sheer misery, but they probably are not learning how to add as well.

If we are going to educate all children together, probably some combination of the two approaches will have to be taught. The more abstract parts of new math might better be set as an enrichment activity for the good math students.

MUSIC AND OTHER LESSONS

We all hear stories about the lad who had to practice the piano four hours a day at age six and composed a symphony at 17. We often wonder how many children were made to practice an instrument for four hours a day at age six and never touched it again as soon as their parents got off their backs.

As in sports, some children have natural talent in music and some don't. And as in sports, those who have a natural talent will probably show it in some way or another. There is no evidence that, if we start one child on an instrument at age six, and start his identical twin on the same instrument at age nine, there will be a difference in performance between the two children at age twelve.

Many young children do not have the finger coordination needed to be good on an instrument. Pushing them too soon results in the same thing that happens when we push him in reading and writing too soon — a sense of failure in the child and a feeling of disappointment in the parent and teacher. Most teachers of music can give the parents an honest impression of the child's talent and whether strong encouragement is a good idea.

It is nice if a child likes music and learns to play an instrument well enough so that it gives him some pleasure and feeling of accomplishment. If a child shows interest in learning an instrument, by all means, get him lessons if you can afford it. But allow him to save face. If he's not enjoying it after five or six lessons, let him quit. If you let him quit, do not express disappointment, but rather tell him that it was good that he learned as much as he did. If he should show renewed interest at a later age, give him another chance. Maybe he wasn't ready for the lessons when he first tried.

Unfortunately many parents and teachers feel that "idle hands are the devil's workshop." Usually, these same adults will value their own leisure time. If you force a child to stay with the lessons, and he does not have the talent or interest, nothing will come of it anyway. All that will result is a waste of both of your time, and a feeling of resentment on the part of the child. Like you, he does not like to be forced into unpleasant situations.

SPEECH PROBLEMS

Speech is how your words sound when you say something, while language is how you think, what you say, what words you use to say it, and how it is understood. Speech requires movement and coordination of muscles. Development of speech involves the maturation of the brain, while the style in which speech is used (dialects, accents, localisms) is a function of the culture in which a child is raised. A child can learn the rules of speech (syntax) very well, although his speech may not sound right because he speaks in a dialect or because of articulation problems. Let us talk briefly of these two areas:

Dialect

One excellent example of dialect is "black language." No matter where they live, many black people use certains forms of language which are common to the black culture, and may well have their roots in African languages. The rules of black language are just as strict and as complicated as are the rules of white language. One language is probably no better or no worse than the other — only different.

As more blacks move into the middle class, they can become *bilingual.* They can speak the language of the white middle class quite well. Some may speak black language at home, or when they become very relaxed. Many blacks can switch their language according to whom they are talking, just like a Frenchman who has lived in this country for a long time can switch between languages.

Articulation

Articulation is how the child pronounces the different sounds needed for his speech. Since all children develop the skill to make sounds through maturation, and since each child matures at his own rate of speed, the children who are slower in this area of maturation have speech problems. Typically these children are boys, since girls usually mature faster than boys.

Many children have not developed the maturity to correctly say the "r", "s", "v", etc., sounds by the time they are in school, and a good number are not able to say those sounds until they are in the third or fourth grade.

This situation is a beautiful example of our madness when it comes to education. Some children are less mature than others in making sounds, so we call them "problem" children and try to *cure* them! Furthermore, since children whose speech is immature tend to be immature in reading and other behaviors, some people go around saying that articulation problems are a sign of emotional disturbance.*

So, many articulation programs were started in the school. And were they successful! By the time many children had three years of speech therapy, they stopped lisping. Of course many would have grown out of their lisping by fourth grade if everybody had left them alone. Some others *never* grow out of their lisp. Most adults with lisps or other articulation problems can be easily understood. It is only when people around them are so intolerant of differences that it becomes a problem.

Finally people started getting wise to the fact that what they were doing would eventually be taken care of by age. Many children may be very good in language, but in their own style. If the day ever comes that we learn to appreciate someone else's style, there may be hope for the world.

AUDITORY DISCRIMINATION

A child may hear something well enough because his hearing is good — he can hear all sound frequencies needed for speech. But some children have problems with *auditory discrimination.* The teacher will say "go to the door" and the child will go to the *drawer.* Young children often will confuse the words "ear" and "year", no matter how clearly it is pronounced. We all have this trouble from time to time, and we suppose that we can all tell embarrassing stories when we did not hear something quite right and did something very foolish. Well, some children have this

---

*We are talking here of the general run of speech problems. A child who, at age 5, is totally unintelligible by even adults who know him, of course requires more specialized services.

problem all of the time. In most cases, they grow out of it, but we have seen adolescents who are still mishearing words.

Any child who consistently misses words should have his hearing checked by an audiologist. If it turns out not to be a hearing loss, there are some tests that can be given to check a child's auditory discrimination. However, most of those tests are not very good for a variety of reasons. The best way that a parent or teacher can spot this is by watching and listening to the child. If you suspect a child is having trouble in discriminating speech sounds, try to figure out what he thought you said, so you know how to correct yourself. But *do not* try asking him to tell you what he thought you said. Children who have this kind of trouble can get quite sensitive about it, and your asking that question can really push him into a corner. Then he has to show you he is stupid because he cannot repeat it — and most children with auditory discrimination problems, as well as their parents and teachers, think they are stupid.

In dealing with a child who does not understand you well, you cannot treat him like he is hard of hearing. For example, you should try to *enunciate* clearly to him, while you should try to talk naturally to a hard of hearing child so he can read your lips more easily. However, it does help to use hand gestures to help him understand, to repeat the important word or words in a sentence so that he has a couple of chances to hear, and to be understanding when he does mishear.

GRADES

It should be fairly clear from our discussion of competition (p. 32) that we are not too sold on the idea of grades. Grades might be more realistic if schools graded children on things that each child can do, rather than grading everybody on the same thing. This would, of course, mean changing the school curriculum to the point that we could try to teach children things they *can* learn with methods they *can* use, rather than teaching them the same old things that schools have never taught successfully in the same old way that has worked for too few children.

The child who has a 140 I.Q. and reads well is less deserving of an A than a child with an 80 I.Q. in many instances. School is a piece of cake for the first child, and, if he can conform despite his boredom, he can be the best student in the class with next to no effort. The child with the 80 I.Q. may have a true desire to learn, but no matter how hard he tries, he won't make it. Is this fair?

Some teachers say they grade children according to their individual ability. We doubt that for two reasons: the teacher seldom knows that child's ability unless he was evaluated by the school psychologist (which is seldom done because there are usually too few psychologists to even see the "problem" cases), and we feel most teachers would be very hesitant about giving an A to the poorest student in the class because he tried so hard.

Schools that give S and U grades (satisfactory and unsatisfactory) are probably better off than those that give A's, B's, C's, D's, and F's, (for some reason, the letter E disappeared from most grading schemes). For one thing, it takes the pressure off the teacher who has to decide between which two children to draw the line between A and B, and between the other grades as well. But even with S and U grades, what does that tell the child, the parents, and next year's teacher?

We feel that a child's progress can best be handled through a series of formal conferences between the teacher and child and the teacher and parent. Occasional short letters to the parents, telling them more where the child is doing *well* than where he is doing poorly can help. In this way, not only is the teacher communicating with the child and the child's parents, but it gives the teacher a chance to point out the nice things about their child to uptight, anxious parents.

This means eliminating grades pretty much. The Center for Educational Reform summarizes some pretty good reasons for this, many given by students:

1. The effect of a grade on a student's life is too great for a single number or letter.
2. Grades come from tests which are designed more for the giving of grades than for evaluating the student.
3. Too many hypocritical factors enter in, like how well the teacher likes the student.

4. Children become concerned about grades, not about evaluating their own performances.
5. Grades interfere with the teaching process. Children are fearful of interacting with a teacher for fear of looking "dumb."
6. The competition for grades become more important than learning.
7. Grades are related to very little of a child's behavior out of the classroom.
8. Children select courses which are easy, instead of interesting or valuable.
9. The anxiety surrounding the possibility of getting bad grades makes learning unpleasant.
10. Grades force the student to dishonesty.
11. Students learn for tests by cramming, which is a very inefficient way to learn. Grades may reduce the amount of learning which can take place.

They conclude: "Change and creation can be precarious tasks, but they are tasks of life. The death of grades may well be the birth of learning."

THE SPECIAL PROBLEMS OF BEING A MINORITY CHILD

A friend of ours, a social worker, took a vacation some years ago. He decided to drive across the southwestern part of the country toward southern California. In a rather remote area, something went wrong with his car — a fan belt, a spark plug, or something else that is in the class of things that go wrong in that mass of mystery below the car hood. This required sending to Los Angeles for the part.

The man was then stuck in a small town for a couple of days. This town was largely made up of poor people. Being a sociable fellow, our friend went around on kind of a busman's holiday. He found that the town was in terrible shape. Unemployment was high. Delinquency was a worry. Girls were getting pregnant while single. The welfare roles were crowded. Kids were dropping out of school. The divorce rate was high. Many of the people were viewed as alcoholic.

A few years later, he was in the same general area and went

back to see some of the people he had met on the earlier visit. He was shocked to find that the town had completely changed. Unemployment was no longer a problem. Children were not being called delinquents anymore, and, if incorrigible, were being sent to private schools where the cost took care of their behavior. Illegitimate pregnancy was down because some of the girls were flying off to Puerto Rico or Japan for abortions. Welfare was almost nonexistent, kids were staying in school, families were staying together, and alcoholism was down.

We have often used this community as an example of how a community can pull itself up by its own bootstraps. Working hard and pulling together really improved the town. Discovering oil beneath the town helped, too.

We are not sure this story is exactly true, but there is much evidence that being poor can cause a group of people more trouble than just about anything else. The children typically have had poor prenatal care, sloppy work at birth, and must often go through truly degrading experiences to get normal health care. (An official of a very large hospital once told us how they treated the black people in the ghetto surrounding the hospital. They had to arrive at 8 A.M. to get treated, and sometimes had to wait until 4 P.M. They had to sit on hard benches while waiting. The staff treated them like animals and the words "nigger" or "savage" were not avoided by some staff members. In all, they were treated with contempt. Was it any wonder, he asked, that Blacks in another nearby ghetto burned down a neighborhood health center while leaving other buildings on the block alone?).

When the minority child gets to school, his troubles continue. The American Indian has probably had the worst time of it. White America considered (and still does) the Indian so inept as a parent that children were forcibly removed from their families and sent to boarding school at age five. There they were punished if they used their tribe's language or customs. This practice is still in effect in many places.

Indians are still taught history from the traditional point of view which tells of the Indian in terms which are negative and often out-right lies. It is very difficult for people to keep their pride in themselves under such conditions. One professional man we know was the only one of twelve children who escaped being sent off to these prisons-in-the-name-of-schooling by being hidden under the bed by his mother when the white officials came for him.

In Minneapolis, Indians are less than one percent of the population, while representing ten percent of the foster children. Of the many licensed foster homes there, only one was an Indian home. We have been involved in many cases where Indian children are committed to foster homes over their parents' protests. Welfare workers are often very unsympathetic to the Indian's feeling of family which, although different than the white man's view, has far closer relationships generally. The children will often escape from their foster homes to go back to their parents. And well it is that at least some do, because Indian husbands and wives tend to drift apart when the children are taken from them.

One of us has been the psychologist for an Indian children and family service project (run by Indians for Indians) for some time now. Indians who were evaluated psychologically tend to have I.Q.'s in the normal range with their performance skills higher than verbal skills, and read quite adequately. They get in trouble more because the school staff doesn't understand their life styles, their values (for example, Indian culture does not stress competition like the Whites and Blacks do), their interests, and their pride. In other words, they *bother* the teacher. Most of the children seen would not, if white, be in trouble.

Blacks and Mexican-Americans have many problems in common. Mexican-American children often come from a home where either they speak Spanish or their parents speak it, and little English is used in the home. Blacks usually speak English only, but their English is different from what we call "standard" or middle-class white English. Black language has a set of rules as rigid as white language. These rules are no better or worse, but they *are* different. For example, the "be" form ("I be there" instead of "I am there") is felt by some black linguists to be directly derived from African language style.

Both Blacks and Mexican-Americans are notoriously poor, not because they have no skills, but because of discrimination (example: A medical school we know tripled—from three to nine

—the number of black freshmen. The number of women admitted dropped by six. Moral: If you want to get into graduate school, be a black woman so they can count you in two quotas). Police are often brutal to minority children, because police come from the lower middle class of Whites, who are always looking over their shoulder at the black and Spanish-speaking peoples who are just below them on the job ladder and always nipping at their heels.

When the minority child gets into trouble he is usually sent away to rehabilitation centers where he learns how to be a better criminal. White children are often sent home.

When minority children get to school, they do not speak exactly the same language as do the teachers. Rather than learning to communicate and deal with each other, they get right into reading instruction. No wonder so many children are doomed to failure. (Doomed is the proper word — the pressures on black youth are so great that, although Blacks overall commit suicide less frequently than Whites, young Blacks, ages 15-24, commit suicide at a higher rate than like-aged Whites).

When new school programs are set up for minority children, they are typically the same old things in new packages. More teachers and other professionals are hired, maybe some expensive machinery is bought, but nothing changes.

Many minority leaders complain that, because of the racism inherent in the school system, their children get shunted aside in favor of white children. For example, if a black and white child are not learning well, the chances are that the Black will be called mentally retarded and the White will be called *learning disabled.* The latter term has much more of a positive image, suggesting that the learning disabled white child is average but needs extra remedial help to fulfill his potential. The black child is seen as inferior and needs much less of a challenge, including much less of the monies set aside for special programs.

The minority child is typically poorly understood by his teachers. At a recent course that we presented, a teacher objected to the speech given by our instructor describing the problems of the minority child. "I see all my children as being exactly the same and I treat them that way," she said. "Groovy," he snapped, "except for one thing. They are *not* all the same, and you had better learn it fast, lady!"

The truth is that their teachers do see them as different, not as individuals but rather different as a group. The school with a large minority population is seen by educators as a "problem" school by definition. The children also see themselves as different from what the teachers want. The minority children feel isolated and *are* isolated in a hostile environment. If they are offered special programs, the end result is often to reinforce their "inferior" image. One example recently encountered was a remedial reading program in a black school. The white teacher was using the subject of manners as the vehicle for teaching. But, in fact, what she did was set herself up as a model, thus illustrating that the manners of black children are wrong.

Many Whites, including their teachers, their principal, their school board members, and the parents of their white schoolmates resent any "special" programs. To some extent, we agree. We feel that there should be no black studies unit, Chicano studies unit, Indian studies unit, or any other special studies program (although they could exist as enrichment programs). These materials *should* be incorporated into the regular curriculum when it is revised so as to reflect reality, and taught to *all* students, just as the minority student is taught about white culture. But until that happy day comes, such programs are needed and should be taught by the people who can relate to such programs.

In addition, it should be recognized that there are other forces at work in the education of minority children. What is the effect on black children who, when studying the traditional view of Lincoln, read in *Ebony* that ". . . the Emancipation Proclamation was not what people think it is and that Lincoln issued it with extreme misgivings and reservations." Old myths must die. The communications media is now so diverse that the *truth* will come from someplace. If it is ignored in the classroom, it may be gotten on the street or on television (poor Blacks probably spend more time than most in front of the television, and regard it as more truthful than some other media). In such a case, the black student may disregard some of the things he learns in school since, if they lied about one thing, what *can* you believe (see discussion of Cognitive Dissonance, pp. 193-195)?

It is our feeling that it is unfortunate, although understandable, that so many minority leaders have bought the white bag. After all, they, too, are propagandized about the goodness of the present educational system. Parent groups in Harlem call for a return to the basic three R's of education, and one of the most prominent black psychologists insists publicly that "further learning is impossible" without reading and mathematics. We feel that there are many other things and other ways to learn (pp. 102-107) and that a more realistic view of the value of academic education in its present form is needed (pp. 88-91).

However, many minority leaders are casting about for other options. Locally, Indian leaders are attempting to provide an Indian school for their children. The Afro-American Educators Conference concluded:

> In each local community black educators must develop a criteria for selection of the materials which will be presented to the Board of Education, to local textbook committees, and to the major publishing houses which provide text and supplemental materials to that community. It is incumbent upon us, if we are to serve this society, that instructional materials which we select be both educationally sound and incorporate a strong black orientation.
>
> Black classroom teachers must help black students to speak the language of the market place and assist them as they move back and forth between "their own thing and a white American thing." Since all groups usually speak two languages, one at home and within their group and another in the economic world; by nurturing and respecting our own language and effectively manipulating the other we will become a truly bilingual people. This is necessary to achieve a viable economic base . . .

It is not only the learning of minority children which must be considered, but their feelings as well. The football coach who calls his black players "niggers" in the coffee room will communicate his hatred for Blacks in other places. The teachers who see all black, brown and red children as "culturally deprived" will communicate it (we can always tell when it is a minority child referred to us, because almost always the problem is described as cultural deprivation).

But there are other areas of insensitivity as well. Christmas programs and carols, which take up the first three weeks in December in some schools, are another problem. Probably 10 to 20 percent of Americans belong to non-Christian religions or are atheists. Not only should they not be forced to participate in Christian Christmas programs in public schools, it is only by not having such programs that those children will not feel singled out.

There is nothing wrong with having some interested children put on a one-shot Christmas program for the whole school, as long as the same thing is routinely done by the followers of Mohammed, Crazy Horse, Malcolm X, Bhudda, Martin Luther King, Confucious, Sitting Bull, and as long as Jews, Mormons, Unitarians, B'hai, etc., are afforded the same chance.

Many teachers do not offend children on purpose. As one recently said to us, when called for using the expression, "Jew" someone down, "I didn't mean anything bad by it. Some of my best friends, etc." Schools should invite leaders from minority groups to come and explain their positions. Maybe then there will be fewer blunders.

In much of this book, we are discussing the problems that can be encountered by white children. Minority children have the same chance of having one or more of these characteristics which can cause problems for the white child. In other words, the probability of the white child's having problems in school is high. Add to this minority status, language differences, and cultural differences, and the pressures on minority children usually become so great as to be overwhelming.

The other factor is that most minority children are poor. Their culture must adapt to their status in a rich society. Society usually downgrades the poor. Is it any surprise that minority children find it difficult to relate to the schools' values of success, achievement, and conformity?

It therefore becomes critical that *all* children be given the dignity and recognition they deserve. It must be recognized that we are all different, and our differences should make us more interesting to each other, rather than a source of scorn.

CHAPTER IV

CURRENT METHODS OF DEALING WITH POOR ACHIEVEMENT

DOES HEADSTART OR KINDERGARTEN MAKE A DIFFERENCE?

There is one very important difference between Headstart programs and kindergarten. In most places, kindergarten is required by law. Headstart is not required, and is aimed primarily at poor children.

In most states children who are five by September 1 are eligible for kindergarten. Most Headstart programs are for children who are one to two years younger.

The main difference between children who go to kindergarten and those who do not is that those who do are better able to "fit in" first grade. In other words, they can sit still a little better, are more hip to the school routine, and may have some reading readiness skills. However, all of these differences disappear during the first grade, and by the end of first grade there is no difference in behavior or school achievement between those who went to kindergarten and those who did not.

As for Headstart, President Nixon wrote in 1970:

"In our Headstart program, where so much hope is invested, we find that youngsters enrolled only for the summer achieve almost no gains, and the gains of those in the program for a full year are soon matched by their non-Headstart classmates from similarly poor backgrounds."

Why don't such programs "work"? Quite possibly it is because both kindergarten and Headstart are hung up on only two goals of education: behavioral conformity and reading.

Most children come to school bright-eyed and bushy-tailed and ready to learn. They have already learned more in their first five years of life than they will ever learn again. But learning in school is very different from out-of-school learning. In school, the language used, the rules and the ways to learn are very different from the free learning of preschool days.

Headstart and kindergarten both try to get the child to conform in his behavior and to make him ready to learn "reading, 'riting, and 'rithmetic". The child is not always ready or interested enough in learning to be ready for this learning. Many children are not mature enough physically for this much rule following, sitting still, or this kind of learning.

Because this is a nation of many peoples, many children are not familiar with the language style, the customs and values taught in the schools. They have heard and learned a different language style, have had different values stressed in their homes and have different cultures than the culture of the school. Mostly these children are Black, Indian and Spanish-American children. Often, however, they are also white children whose parents are poor.

Despite what we like to believe, the United States has very strong class distinctions based on money. Schools are mostly taught by people who are not necessarily in the middle or upper classes. However, they teach the culture of the most powerful classes of the society. The end result is that what is done in the school is strange for a large number of our children.

Headstart and kindergarten programs are supposed to help children to be ready for this strange, new experience. However, since the schools have always had very narrow standards for learning, behavior, language style and values, these programs expect to change the children to fit into the school mold. The basic idea behind Headstart seems to be a belief that children who differ from what the school demands of them are in some way inferior, rather than different. The children are called culturally disadvantaged or culturally deprived. In reality, the children often have very rich cultures in their homes and neighborhoods, but are culturally *different* from the white middle-class.

Because the goals of Headstart and kindergarten are to change the child and give him "culture," they frequently fail. No real efforts are made to accept the child as having a different and valuable culture. The effort is always directed to teach the child to speak "correctly" and behave "correctly" according to middle-class attitudes of what is correct.

Some children speak a form of nonstandard English which works nicely for them in their homes and neighborhoods. Some children speak a different language at home, and do not understand the language of the school. These children are told that the way they speak is not correct, but little effort is made to teach the child English as a second language which, for them, it is. The child then struggles to understand what he is doing wrong and to understand what will please the teacher.

Children learn best from people who understand them, can tolerate them, and seem interested in them. In this way, they are just like adults. A good example is found among the Amish people in this country. Children in Amish schools, with Amish teachers who have 8th grade educations, do better on achievement tests than Amish children in public schools where the teachers are college graduates.

Kindergarten and Headstart programs are seen as failures when the children who attend them do not show improved achievement in grade school. This improved achievement is usually measured by how well the child can read when compared to other children. This really does not tell us much about what the child has learned, only how well he has learned to read. Sometimes children are compared to see if their I.Q. scores are higher after Headstart or kindergarten. Since I.Q. tests are also unfair to children who are not white and middle-class, there is little change seen (see pp. 28-30).

There is one very good thing about Headstart. The poor children get a hot lunch, and in some places, a breakfast. Since many children whose families are poor are not well fed, the lunch program can be very helpful.

Since Headstart and kindergarten have failed, now many

people figure we can begin failing one to two years sooner. Some people are now talking about making school compulsory at age two. Is their goal teaching or brainwashing? For many children, these years could be better spent looking at clouds, riding a trike, or watching earthworms in their back yard.

The middle-class equivalent of headstart is the nursery school. In October of 1970, the U.S. Office of Education reported that 40 percent of pre-school aged children now attend pre-school. Probably most of the increase is accounted for by children who are not poor. This increase reflects the desire of middle-class parents to remake their children into the American Dream. Dr. Edward Zigler, chief of the U.S. Office of Child Development, expressed concern:

> What is troublesome to me about the vast increase in nursery-school enrollment is that much of it is accounted for by middle-class children whose parents believe that nursery school experience will result in increased I.Q. and later school achievement for their children.

Since about half of mothers of school-age children work, some form of day care is obviously needed for them. Many Headstart and Nursery School programs are now in existence where the philosophy is changing. More and more, they are trying to make the experience fun, while providing enough stimulation for the children to learn on their own.

It is not the presence of pre-school programs to which we object. It is rather the goals of some of them — the shut-up, sit down, and learn to read philosophy — which we feel is off-base.

Children at this age are neither ready nor interested in formal school. What do we want from the children? Why must children be such an ego trip for some parents?

AT WHAT AGE SHOULD A CHILD START SCHOOL?

We will not go into detail on this question. It has been covered beautifully by Louise Bates Ames of the Gesell Institute in her book, *Is Your Child in the Wrong Grade?* It is very important because the Gesell people feel that probably more than one third of all children are doing school work which is too rough for them at their present state of physical maturation.

Most school districts have a legal starting age. Usually, all children who are five before September 1 of that year will start kindergarten. Although all are the same age, there are great differences in maturation, coordination, and other forms of behavior.

Dr. Ames points out what most kindergarten teachers learn very quickly: that boys are less mature than girls by about six months or more. In other words, although both boys and girls are the same age in kindergarten, most boys *look* and *act* younger than most girls.

Dr. Ames makes the case that, for many children, holding them out of school for an additional year or having them repeat a grade might help. She points out that children are "babied" not *because* parents want to baby them, but that parents tend to protect "babyish" children. Other points she raises about holding a child out of school:

1. He is not going to "catch up" in a year if he is immature.
2. It probably will not hurt him emotionally; in fact, it will probably be easier on him if he can do more of the work.
3. If a child repeats, it is true that other kids may make fun of him. But if the reasons for repeating are explained to him, that it was done — not because he is "dumb" — but for his sake, he will be able to get by. Besides, which is worse: being teased for being held back when the child is doing better work, or being teased for doing poor work when he is in the right grade?
4. Ignore physical size. It may mean something today, but today's big boy may be passed up by many in a couple of years.

So, if you have any question about your child, hold him out of kindergarten for a year. If he is very good in school work he can always skip a grade later. Besides, research shows that there is no difference between younger and older children in school achievement at upper grade levels. Certainly, maturity plays a strong role in school functioning up until adolescence, but whether the child is older or younger than his classmates makes little difference by the time junior high is reached.

On the other side of the question is the child who misses the cut-off date for entering kindergarten but is so mature that it seems a waste to keep him (or, more often, her) out of school for a year. For this child, many school districts will allow a child who is underage by one or two months to enter school on the recommendations of a school psychologist. Children are selected based upon a high school aptitude (I.Q.), good readiness for reading and writing skills, and being socially and emotionally mature.

Parents often misinterpret the early entrance program. They often feel that it means that their child *passes* a test. This is wrong. The psychologist should recommend only certain children to start early, and then only when based on a complete evaluation of the child's growth and development. Children who are *very* mature for their age quickly learn to fit in with children who are, on the average, six to eight months older than they are.

DO BOYS AND GIRLS LEARN THE SAME WAY?

An interesting thing happened when they started building I.Q. tests. In choosing the tasks to include in most tests, they took those tasks on which boys and girls did equally well, on the average, and threw out those tasks which were done better by one sex than another. Later, there were many studies printed in the professional literature which showed that boys and girls do equally well on I.Q. tests. This would be like choosing only short children and then saying, "See, boys and girls are the same height."

Sex differences in learning show up in kindergarten, although they are obvious long before then. On the average, girls mature more rapidly than boys. Although there are great individual differences, girls appear to be, on the average, about six months to a year advanced over boys when beginning school. They are taller, have developed more of their speech sounds, are better coordinated, etc.

Their interests differ, too. During the readiness training in kindergarten, girls tend to learn their letters more easily than numbers while boys learn their numbers more easily than letters. Maybe this is one reason why, when older, girls do better, on

the average, in literature and the arts and boys do better in math
and more precise studies.

This is proven to some extent by the facts on later behavior.
More boys have trouble with reading than do girls. Typically,
there are four to ten times as many boys as girls in remedial
reading classes. Because their impulse control (see pp. 162-163)
matures more slowly, most children described as behavior problems in school are boys.

Because girls have better coordination with their fingers,
writing may be easier for them than it is for boys. This kind of
coordination, called *fine motor coordination,* is superior for girls
throughout life. Thus, if you need brain surgery, you would
probably do best to select a female surgeon, if only they would
let girls into medical school.

Girls seem to do better in all language type tasks, even when
they do not involve using the mouth. Colin McAdam, of the
Faribault School for the Deaf, feels that girls even learn sign
language easier than do boys.

Many people say that the reason that boys have more problems in elementary school is because most elementary school
teachers are women. These people say that boys need a "male
image" to identify with and they will learn better. We think
this is nonsense. We feel that one other sex difference is that
women are often more able to stand little children over long
periods of time than can men. Of course, there are exceptions.
For this reason, in selecting teachers, we should not talk of men
versus women, but rather we should ask *which* man and *which*
woman.

HOW TO RAISE A CHILD'S I.Q.

It has already been shown that the I.Q. score predicts school
success. It is a *relative* score, so I.Q. tests are *built* to have 50
percent of children score below the middle and 50 percent to
score above this point.

There have been many studies, costing millions of dollars of
tax monies, which show that this program or that program will
raise I.Q., sometimes as much as ten points. (The famous Swiss
psychologist, Dr. Piaget, is reported to have commented on

programs to raise I.Q.'s: "Only the Americans would *try*.") Unfortunately, there are other studies which have shown that this gain does not last much longer than the study, and once the study is over, the children start to drop back to their earlier I.Q. score.

You can do what the experiments described in these studies frequently do, which is basically to teach the children how to take I.Q. tests. Go to the library, get some books on psychological tests, and look up the Stanford-Binet and Wechsler Intelligence Tests. Most text books give some examples of items so you can teach the child these items and that should be enough to raise his I.Q.*

Of course, this rise in I.Q. should have absolutely *no* effect on his school work. Since the I.Q. test only tells you how a child *should* do in school (but the tests ignore his reading skills which are also important), tampering with the test will not affect his school work. It would be like changing the gas gauge when your car's tank is empty. Your gauge may tell you the tank is full, but your tank just isn't full.

In fact, "helping" a child in this way can be harmful. If you artificially raise his I.Q., everyone will expect more of him than he can give. You might do better to tell him to do a little less than his best on such tests, so that his schoolwork is a little *better* than the test indicates. Then he would be called an "overachiever" and everyone would praise the teacher and parents.

DOES REMEDIAL READING HELP?

It was pointed out above that "average" reading level means the point where 50 percent of children score above and 50 percent of children score below. We *cannot* select one point in the middle of a range of scores and say that everyone should hit it. If we want to select women of average height for a job, and the average height for women is 5'4", we cannot insist they *all*

---

*As a matter of fact, some schools are doing this as a matter of course now. We've noted that many schools are buying, among their educational materials, some games and exercises which are strangely familiar. Most common are some like a test using blocks. Some companies must be making materials which are very much like those on I.Q. tests.

be 5'4". We could try to stretch out the legs of the 50 percent of women who are shorter but this would be at least an expensive and inconvenient way of doing it.

But when educators start insisting that all children read at "grade level", this means that they somehow want to crowd 100 percent of the children into a place where only 50 percent *can* fit. This is, of course, impossible.

What would happen if we took 100 fourth grade children who represented all levels of skill in reading? As described above, 50 percent would read above grade level and 50 percent would read below grade level. Now, what if we took 25 of those who read below grade level and, through remedial reading, got them to the point where these 25 kids were above grade level? The school district would build "local norms" (see pp. 40-41) which would again force 25 children *below* grade level. Thus, the whole idea of getting *all* children to read at grade level is pretty silly.

What happens in studies of remedial reading is probably just as silly. There have been thousands of studies of remedial reading. They all go pretty much the same way. A group of below average readers is selected and half of them are given remedial reading and half are not. At the end of the remedial reading course, both groups are given a reading test. Almost always, the group that had remedial reading scores much higher than the group that didn't. (One often gets a sneaking suspicion that many of those studies in which this *does not* happen just don't wind up being published in professional journals. After all, most of these studies are done by professors who teach remedial reading.)

Given these good results, all school districts then develop remedial reading programs and almost everybody is happy. New remedial reading teachers are hired, some become supervisors, and parents are happy that the school is doing something. Only the kids are miserable because now they have an extra half hour or hour a day of reading lessons, and since they are not good at reading, they don't like it.

In 1969, we published a couple of articles in the *Journal of Learning Disabilities*. What we did was to look for those studies that went back some time *after* the end of remedial reading to see what happened. We found seven such studies, most done outside the U.S. All showed the same thing. Children do not stay at the same level in reading — they improve. In these seven studies, the children improved at about the same rate that they had been going *before* remedial reading. In other words, if a group of children in grade 4.0 were reading at grade 3.2, they had been picking up .8 of a grade during each grade. Let us say that after one year of remedial reading, in grade 5.0, they were reading at grade 5.0, a pick-up of 1.8 years in one year. This almost always happens. Maybe it is because remedial reading teaches children how to take reading tests, a skill which does not seem to stay with them long. However, in those studies which went back, let us say, two years later (in grade 7.0) it was found that the children still were achieving at an increase of .8 a year or, in other words, were reading at grade 5.6 in grade 7.0.

In 1970, President Nixon was discussing the effects of the almost one billion dollars sunk into remedial reading programs of Title I, and said,

> . . . before-and-after tests suggest that only 19 percent of the children in such programs improve their reading significantly; 15 percent appear to fall behind more than expected, and more than two thirds of the children remain unaffected — that is, they continue to fall behind.

Thus, don't expect any miracles from remedial reading. If remedial reading allows the child to go to a small group and do poorly in reading, it is certainly better than having him do poorly in front of 30 youngsters in the regular class. Unfortunately, all too often they have to do both.

DOES PERCEPTUAL-MOTOR TRAINING WORK?

Some years ago, researchers became very interested in measuring *perceptual-motor functioning*. When we can see or hear something correctly, *perception* is whether our brain correctly interprets that something once we have seen or heard it.

Perceptual-motor functioning was usually measured by showing the child a picture of a geometric form, like a triangle or a line of dots, and having him copy it (the copying was the motor— or movement—part of it). Sometimes they traced forms or tried to draw after the picture was taken away. But just about always, these tests involved copying geometric designs.

One other thing that was found was that poor readers did more poorly on these tests than good readers. Pretty soon a lot of people started claiming that the reason a child read poorly was *because* he had poor perceptual-motor coordination. This naturally led to the popularity of therapy programs. These therapy programs were to improve the child's perceptual-motor coordination. If he was better in that, he would be better in reading, or so the thinking went.

These programs became very popular and many different people do "perceptual training" or "perceptual-motor training" now.

There was only one thing wrong with their logic. True, perceptual training programs greatly helped the child's score on the test of perceptual-motor functioning, but it had no effect on his reading.

Statisticians have long been saying that "correlation does not mean causation." In other words, just because kids who are high on one test have a better chance of being high on the second test, this does not mean that both tests are measuring exactly the same thing. But educators continue making the same mistakes. For example, we noted in another section that poor readers usually have more areas of immaturity than good readers. Recently, someone found that poor readers had poorer balance than good readers. This is not surprising because balance improves with maturation. So, guess what? They started a remedial balancing program!

One aspect of perceptual-motor functioning which is almost always noted is *reversals*. This is when the child flops the drawings over so that they are pointed the opposite way. In reading, we see it when a child sees the letter "d" and reads it "b." We know one child who is kind of a super-reader. She did not read when she got to first grade and by the time she finished first grade she was scoring somewhere around the middle of the fourth grade in reading skills on most tests.

However, every time she wrote, she almost always reversed many letters, including g, q, b, d, p, e, a, etc. Nevertheless, she reversed when she wrote but almost *never* when she read.

So even though reading words and writing words seem to involve the same brain functions, they don't necessarily. By the way, the child described above always scored superior on tests of perceptual-motor functioning, because she could copy geometric forms well. She just had trouble remembering which way letters went.

WHAT HAPPENS TO THE CHILD WHO DOESN'T READ WELL?

It is not surprising, during the first three or four years of school, that the poor reader does not like school. What really surprised us was that when we met parents of children who read poorly, many told us that their child loves school. Closer questioning usually reveals that these children love the social parts of school, like the play ground or lunch.

Most children who do not do well in school hate it. Every year it costs New York City schools three million dollars for vandalism, most of it being broken school windows. You show us a school window breaking and we'll show you an unsuccessful student throwing the stone.

At home, he gets a lot of heat from his parents: "Try harder!" or "You can't go out on Fridays unless you raise your grades" and other such statements.

Unfortunately, parents have been dragged into the school craze. They are always being blamed because their kids do badly in school. It should be no surprise to parents. Many parents did not do well in school either. (There's an old proverb: "The apple doesn't fall far from the tree").

Children who read poorly are under a lot of stress. Every day they must face going to school where both the teacher and other kids *know* they cannot read. And it is very hard to "con" such youngsters. So often, during psychological evaluations of such children, they tell us they are dumb or stupid. Some children would rather be seen as a behavior problem than as a stupid youngster. They will act up in class, either out of boredom (if a child can't do the work, what *can* he do with his time?) or in an attempt to avoid doing the work (it's sometimes easier to be a bad boy than a stupid boy).

For such children, there is usually no one to turn to. Their parents are hostile, their teachers see their failure to learn as reflecting poorly on their teaching job, and the other kids who are lucky enough to do well in school often do not want to be tainted by associating with them. Either they are isolated or are forced to be friends with the other "dumb" kids.

Most delinquents are poor school achievers (see pp. 144-145). Many of these children are no doubt pushed into delinquency. There self-image becomes so bad that there doesn't seem to be much reason to try to conform.

Typical of what is done was a six year study of 400 "potentially delinquent" high school girls in New York City. They were given group and individual therapy by social workers, but no good came of it except that the program made the social workers feel better.

In other words, you cannot spend eight or nine years of a child's life making him a failure and then expect to "cure" him at age 15 or 16. If new programs are not started at a young age, and are not programs which will make the child feel like a success, then forget it.

This is not new. Kramer, in his book *History Begins at Sumer,* tells us of the nonachiever 4,000 years ago in the ancient civilization:

> Wayward, disobedient, and ungrateful children were the bane of their parents thousands of years ago as well as today. They roamed the streets and boulevards and loitered in public squares, perhaps even in gangs. . . . They hated school and education and made their fathers sick to death with their everlasting gripes and complaints.

In the ancient writings of Sumer, one young man was described who was late to school, was caned for talking and walking out of the gate. Is there anything new under the sun?

When the poor reader grows up (if he grows up — teenage suicide seems to mount as school pressure rises), he is still in big trouble. It is difficult for him to get jobs. First of all, he probably left school before finishing because he was so miserable and could not do the work. There is a great deal of evidence that many industries require high school diplomas when there is absolutely no need for one on the job. Then, in order to find the job, he often has to go through want ads, which require reading. In order to get the job, he has to fill out a job application blank. Many job application blanks are written as a work of art by the personnel manager, but are so hard to read that poor readers often cannot fill them out (words like "domicile" are used instead of "address", directions are given in obscure language, etc.).

If our friend was lucky enough to have someone help him find the job, and then was smart enough to take the application blank home and return it later after he has had help filling it out, he may get the job. Still, people are not understanding. We have heard of cases where there was no reading needed on the job, but where all information to the employee is given in print. In another case, an excellent mechanic kept getting fired from jobs because he could not read the orders well, which took less than five percent of his time and could have been done for him by his supervisor.

The dependence on reading can become so great that someone in a government agency that is supposed to get people jobs once told us how bad it can be. They sent out letters to clients, telling them when to come in for help. If the person did not show, that agency dropped them because they did not think the client showed enough interest. It never occurred to this agency that some of their clients could not read the letter which was written to them in official government jargonese.

In all these cases, all that is really needed is extra understanding. Suggestions for the child in school are covered on pp. 103-107. Making records is now so cheap that little records are stuck into cereal boxes for prizes. Tape recorders are cheap. Good readers can read to poor readers. The written word is not holy. With some extra effort and understanding, people like these can fit into the world. There is *no* reason to exclude them.

What happens to the inefficient reader grown up? Many things can happen. We remember one judge who was sentencing a racketeer to a year in prison. This racketeer had been running a complicated and widespread business for many years, and actually controlled the town. The judge told the racketeer that, ahem, maybe he could spend his year in prison learning to read and write. How pompous!

SPEED READING

There have been many claims that people can be taught to read at fantastic rates. Most people appear to read somewhere between 100 and 400 words a minute, with girls generally reading faster than boys. Some people claim that they can get people up to 10,000 words a minute. This is nonsense. What is happening is that people are being taught to skim — briefly glancing at passages just to get the idea of what is written. The more skimming that takes place, the less the reader understands and remembers details of what is read.

There are ways to get people to increase their reading speed, but only within limits. If the person who reads 200 words a minute can be moved up to 300, or the person who reads 400 words a minute is moved up to 550, these are true improvements and benefits. College reading laboratories have worked on such methods for years and have been successful in raising reading speed without losing understanding of what is read.

Improving the speed of reading within these limits is based on the fact that most people are sloppy in reading. When the eyes move across a line of print, they move in hops, stopping briefly in one spot where one or several words are seen, and hopping on to the next stop, where one or more new words are seen. These stops are called *fixations,* and your speed of reading largely depends on how many fixations there are on a line of reading, and how long the eyes are fixated.

Most people do not keep their eyes moving at a steady speed, but may fixate longer than necessary at one spot, or may look back to a spot earlier on the line or on the line above. This is what slows reading down.

You can be trained to keep your eyes moving at a regular rate and thus speed up your reading. How fast you can go depends on several things, including the size of your vocabulary, how much you knew about the materials you are reading *before* you started reading them, how interested you are in the materials you are reading, your eye coordination, the ease or difficulty *for you* of the materials you are reading, how much you like to read, and how fast you can translate printed words into thoughts.

One simple technique is to keep your finger in the middle of the page and move it down the page at an even rate. If this rate of moving your finger is faster than you normally go, it may keep your eyes moving in the right direction without going back. This alone may significantly raise your speed of reading.

But the most important thing about the speed of reading is called *flexibility*. This means that you should not read everything at the same speed. Should a child read a textbook, a novel, and a poem all at the same speed? The textbook will be slow because the words are difficult. The poem may be slow because the reader may dwell on some lovely phrase or image. The novel may move fast until the youngster gets to the sexy part, where the speed of reading will again slow down.

Again, to talk of everyone reading at the same speed ignores individual differences. There will always be some super readers, some very slow word-by-word readers, and all kinds of variations in between.

HOMEWORK

Most adults work about eight hours a day. Many white collar workers and housewives work less. Many teachers work less. For some reason, many of them feel that their children should put in ten or twelve hours a day on schoolwork. Most homework is make-work, based on the idea that if doing a problem once is good, doing the same type of thing over and over must be better.

Seldom is there a reason that formal homework should be assigned, except for the reason that children have *always* had homework. But are the old ways always the best ways? Research indicates that the achievement level of children is *not* improved by homework.

Maybe if we didn't load the kids down with homework, they would have more time to learn — to learn how to act, to learn about what is going on in the world, etc. We have never

seen one youngster who, after going through the ritual of doing
a book report on one of those dull books called "classics," was
ever turned on to read other old books. Doing 60 addition problems at home sure doesn't excite a child about addition.

If a teacher cannot teach what she wants to teach in six
hours, why not either try something else to teach or some other
way of teaching it? Except in a few cases where children would
do outside work anyway (because they are interested), homework is a failure.

SHOULD A PARENT WORK WITH A CHILD AT HOME?

For some reason, a strange thing can happen at a parent-
teacher conference. After the professional teacher has not taught
the child to read well after working at it for several weeks of
six-hour days, she will tell the parent to work with the child at
home. How the parent, who is not a teacher, is supposed to do
this is not clearly explained.

Not only is the parent not professionally trained to teach,
but both the parent and child are not emotionally ready for
school at home. After failing in front of the teacher all day, the
child is not really excited about the chance to fail in front of
one of his parents for an hour or two at night. Since his parents
are the most important people in the world to him, this is really
rough on him.

In the meantime, the parent gets frustrated. He is not really
turned on with the idea of spending an hour or two a night with
Dick and Jane. Soon he begins to talk that way himself ("See
Daddy Mad? Hate, Daddy, Hate"). But the parent knows that
if he does not work with the child, he will look like he does not
care about the child's work. So usually they end up fighting
with each other and there is a lot more tension in the home.

If the parents really think about it, there is another reason
why, in many cases, one or both of them are the least likely people
to work with their child. Research shows that problems with
reading tend to run in families. In our experience, if the father
cannot read well, there is a good chance that his sons won't
read well, and a smaller chance that his daughters won't read

well. If the mother does not read well, it seems like most or all of her children do not read well.

Sometimes, when we are speaking to a parents' group, especially in a richer neighborhood where the parents are leaning hard on their kids to learn, we pull a bit of a fast one. We tell the parents to go up to the attic, pull out their old report cards and hang them on the refrigerator as an inspiration to their children. This is always met with embarrassed laughter.

Especially for the child who is having trouble with his reading, the parent should leave him alone and give him a rest from school work when he gets home. Home should be the friendly and loving place to go, not another hated school house.

If the parent really wants to be helpful, and if the parent can read well, the parent could spend some time reading assignments aloud to the inefficient reader so that the youngster has some idea of what is going on in the classroom. But this should not be set up as another class at home. The parent should tell the child he is available for this, but the child has to do the asking. And when the child does ask, the parent has to hold up his end of the bargain.

DOES THE TEACHER MAKE A DIFFERENCE IN SCHOOL ACHIEVEMENT?

Pity the poor teacher. In recorded history, the teacher started out as a slave who was particularly good in school learning. His role was to teach the master, his sons, and a few other select slaves. In those days, knowledge of the arts and letters was the sign of the cultured man, and served to separate him from two icky groups, the lower classes and women.

Through the ages, people recognized that education was not as much a tool for improving the lot of human beings, but rather was a tool to keep the rich that way and to keep the poor in their place.

During the middle ages, religion was an important factor in making education a tiny bit more available, but it was not until about 100 years ago in this country that a public education became available. True, it usually was available for only a short while to the poor, and the rich continued to educate *their* children in private schools. But a few of the masses who were particularly good in school made it through school. Seldom did they join the upper classes. More often they became teachers. But not too many people realized that, and thus the American Dream was born.

Even during most of the past 100 years teachers have been little more than slaves. Their behavior, morality, and interests were under constant watch and there was little reward, either in terms of fun or money, for their efforts.

Although we have no statistics on it, it appears that men tutored the rich, while women taught the public school children. Teaching, because the pay and working conditions were so bad, was largely a female occupation. Even more recently, the number of male teachers was so small that in many cities many or most of the school principals were women.

It was probably the Soviet launch of Sputnik which changed all that. Americans, facing the international situation as if it were the Big Ten Football race, realized that they were not number one. Loud voices were raised to improve the learning of basic skills in the schools, while those educators who called for humanity in schools fell silent.

This resulted in 4 things:

1. An increase in pay for teachers, followed by a rise in the number of men involved.

2. A change in the make-up of schools, where women were now teachers and men were coaches or administrators.

3. An increase in the pressure on children to compete in fields which were hard for them.

4. The training of so many engineers that now the market is glutted with them.

Teachers came under more and more pressure to succeed with their students. School systems increased the number of administrators to help the teacher, and these make-work practices resulted in some school systems looking like they need two people (usually men) downtown at the administration building for every teacher (woman) on the firing line. Men often rise to the top in the school bureaucracy by becoming coaches (and incidentally teachers), then counselor, then assistant principal (disciplinarian), principal, and then administrator, as if these were all line operations. These are the people who control the teachers.*

Parents also began pressuring the teachers to improve their children's education so that the children could grow up to be something more than their parents, a sad commentary on the self-image of American parents.

But teachers are not equipped to meet the challenge. They attend college for four years where they take courses taught by professors who often have not been near a classroom for years (if ever), seldom teach children, and who tell teachers how to teach children. (In our graduate days, there were students in education who, after the professor told how to teach kids, pushed him to the edge of his control with such questions as "What if that doesn't work?").

During their last year of teacher's college, they are given about four months of practice teaching in a school. This usually takes place under the direction of a veteran teacher who teaches as she has been taught. Then the practice teacher goes on to the job and teaches as *she* was taught. And every other summer, in order to get a pay raise, in many school districts the teacher has to go back to the college and take more courses. In other words, getting a raise often depends on the ability to sit through college classes instead of improving what goes on in the classroom.

This is the situation the teacher faces when hit with the

---

*Since there are obviously going to be administrators in school systems, we have often wondered if it couldn't be done more fairly. Why not have principalships and other administrative jobs on a rotating basis, so that no administrator gets too far from the classroom? We remember a quote in the newspaper recently, on the occasion of a superintendent's retiring, "I've been away from the classroom for 35 years but it's still my first love." If he loved it so much, why didn't he go back there? The higher you go in promotions in the schools, the further you are from the kids. It would be nice if a teacher knew she could get away from the classroom for 2 years and go downtown and be a curriculum director, as long as she knew she didn't have to stay there. Let them put their experience and knowledge about children into use as an assistant superintendent, as head of the lunch program, as personnel director, and other jobs which seem to be the rewards that many school systems hold out for their best teachers, thus rewarding a good teacher by removing him from teaching.

idea of teacher "accountability" (see pp. 81-82). Then there is the question of whether a teacher *can* make a difference. Since, as we pointed out on pp. 40-41, only 50 percent *can* score above grade level, and children seem to do pretty much the same in school no matter what happens to them, it is a tough situation.

Some educators have been pushing the idea lately that teachers do make a difference in terms of classroom achievement. For example, the author of the famous Coleman report testified before Congress. He pointed out that, in his study, teachers who scored highest on a verbal test were in schools where children had the highest achievement. In research, we must interpret this in terms of what we call a *confounding variable*. These same teachers were also paid more and taught in richer suburbs. It then stands to reason that these suburban districts could outbid other districts and hire teachers who did best in school because they had good verbal skills. Also, rich suburban districts tend to score higher because there are no poor and minority children in the school (see pp. 53-59). In other words, teachers who score the highest are hired by schools where the kids score the highest. Thus, to say that teachers with higher verbal scores are better teachers is like saying that dogs eating grass *causes* it to rain.

Other factors studied include teacher pay, experience, education, etc. None of them make a difference in school achievement. Why? Should we ignore the teacher's influence on learning?

Not at all. The questions raised above are beautiful examples of what is wrong with most educational research. First of all, what is the standard of teacher quality? Scores on achievement tests, that's what. In many cases, it is not even standard achievement tests, but plain old reading tests. Is this what a teacher is supposed to be doing, teaching children how to take achievement tests? The second problem seems to be the unspoken threat that, if we learn what a good teacher is, we can then train all teachers to act like that. Not only do we want to make all children alike, but we want to make teachers alike, too.

Can't we consider other things, too? How about the teacher whose children love her — children who feel happy and proud of themselves for a year? Can we measure that? What about the teacher who tolerates the individual differences in her children, and teaches them according to their need, instead of according to the needs of a reading test? Can we measure that? What about the teacher who develops in a child a curiosity and interest in learning about some particular thing which may stay with them as a source of joy all their life? Can we measure that? What about the teacher who can influence other teachers to be more realistic about *their* children? Can we measure that? What about the teacher who is a friend and advisor to the students? Can we measure that? What about the teacher who provides some success experiences for children who never had success? Can we measure that? For some children, a warm accepting teacher is their only hope.

Some things we can measure. We have a friend, a distributive education teacher, whose students often will spontaneously chip in to buy him a gift, or do favors for him out of school, and seek his advice after they have left school. We *can* measure that, but nobody will.

WHAT IS TEACHER "ACCOUNTABILITY"?

Many school districts are now insisting that achievement test scores be publicized in order to see how well their teachers are teaching the children. A teacher is held "accountable" to make all of her children read at grade level or above. In fact, in some plans, they will be paid according to how their classes do on achievement tests, and achievement tests require reading. *Since only 50 percent of the children can read at grade level or above,* (see pp. 40-41) *an impossible task is created. All* teachers have to fail with a sizable number of students. Trying to get *all* children to score above the 50th percentile is, by definition, a statistical impossibility. Of course, it has been shown that if you choose the right tests (tests that tend to score high), teach the children the materials that are on the test, or a combination of the two, you can *appear* to dramatically raise the scores of certain subgroups of children. However, such artificial gains do little but temporarily mask the problem.

To the embarrassment of the government, this use of tests has been demonstrated in "Performance Contracting." James

Welch of the American Educational Research Association, tells us how it works, and the dangers:

> This is the year of accountability. More specifically, it is the year of performance contracting in education.
>
> Hundreds of school districts across the country are either negotiating such contracts or seriously considering this new idea, which calls for private education-technology firms to be paid only if they produce, with the size of their payments scaled to how quickly and effectively they teach basic skills and raise the grade level of low-performing children.
>
> Amid all this activity, however, it has become clear that the pioneer experiment in performance contracting, a program in Texarkana, Ark., funded by the Office of Education, is in very serious trouble. In brief, independent evaluators have told Texarkana school officials that the private contractor taught the students to take the tests. So many test questions were contaminated by prior teaching that much of the performance measured in the spring must be considered invalid, said the evaluators.

CLASS SIZE

One of the best selling points that schools use to gain acceptance for new programs is that it will result in a smaller sized class. People like the idea of their children getting more personal attention and it usually can make the teacher feel much happier.

Class size has always been based on other than educational reasons. For example, special classes for educably retarded children are usually set at 15 or less. The reason for this, it is reported, goes back to the school administrator in Massachusetts who was writing the first special class laws. Knowing that the average class in his district was 30 children, he figured that half of that would be a good number. And that is why special classes are 15 children.

There is no evidence that smaller classes raise school achievement. Many of us know adults who did well despite large classes in overcrowded urban or parochial schools. On the other hand, it is rumored that Madison Avenue and Wall Street are both run by boys from one room school houses in Minnesota, Iowa, and Wisconsin.

Does class size make *no* difference? Probably, it does make a difference, but in things we find hard to measure. For example, a teacher has to crack down harder on a large class to make sure that they do not get out of control. It is tougher to control 40 than 30 kids, especially if you are trying to work with ten of them in a reading group. Teachers *can* get away with this. Being very strict with a whole class to keep it under control can keep them quiet. But, if there is a school like that in your neighborhood, go sit outside some day at three o'clock. All that stored up energy and frustration breaks loose as soon as they are out of doors. Fighting, running, and general hyperactivity is the rule.

Teachers can work more easily and naturally with small groups. But, in terms of what the youngsters learn, there is no difference if the same old thing is taught in the same old way, even if it is on a one-to-one basis. Teachers can also work with large groups easily, if the things being taught turn the children on.

We are happy to see the trend toward changing ideas about classes. Rooms with a certain number of children in them are for administrative convenience, not for educational convenience. Open schools, where children move between groups of different sizes according to what is being done in the groups, make sense. A teacher can teach several hundred children at once, if a film is being shown or a lecture being given. She probably does best with one or a few children if she is offering advice on a project that only these children are working on. No teacher is needed if a youngster is working by himself.

SEATING ARRANGEMENTS IN CLASS

Most teachers and parents prefer one of two arrangements of seats in a classroom: either the box style of straight rows of equal length, or an incomplete circle, like this:

```
         x x x x x x x x x x x x
                               x
(teacher) X                    x
                               x
                             x x x
         x x x x x x x x x x x
```

Both these arrangements have certain desirable qualities. First of all, they look neat if the principal or a parent arrives. Most principals and parents feel that a neat classroom is a good class-room. Second, it leaves the teacher in a spot where her authority is emphasized by her position in the front and center.

But such arrangements do not seem to be best for children. Classrooms should *not* have bolted-down chairs. The teacher might find that she can arrange the room in terms of the children's needs, rather than in the old way. For example, distract-able children's desks should be against the wall in a blank corner. Children who have difficulties in language should be near the teacher so that she can give them some extra help, a small group of quiet and cooperative children might be able to move their desks near each other and work together. A child who reads well may be in the hall with a couple of nonreaders, reading books to them.

One of the most effective classrooms we have seen had eliminated desks altogether. The floors were carpeted so that children could work together in groups merely by sitting down on the floor. A couple of tables were available in quiet, isolated corners for writing assignments or quiet work. A large refrigerator carton was available for the child who wanted to isolate himself from the stimulation by crawling into it for a few quiet minutes. Each child had his own small drawer for storing his own property.

This means that the public has to change its view of the teachers. The teacher should seldom act as the Queen in the room, dropping words of wisdom to her subjects. Instead, she should act more like guest expert, moving around the room and providing information to the children so that they can learn, in-stead of being taught.

DOES THE SHAPE OF THE SCHOOL MAKE A DIFFERENCE?

In the old days, schools looked pretty much alike. A city school was a box with a playground next to it while a country school was a smaller box and there was playground all around it.

Now, in order to be progressive, new shapes are here. We call these shapes "experimental." We have round buildings and square buildings, high buildings and single-story buildings, snail-shaped buildings and hexagons or pentagons, windowless buildings versus glass buildings, schools dependent on reducing distracting stimuli to a minimum, and schools which have no walls so that children can wander to whatever distracts them. The experimental programs within their walls display an equal variety of forms and colors. Despite the millions of dollars which are spent on these nonexperimental experiments, no controlled studies are reported to determine whether any of these many shapes are any better than any other shape.

It is probably not the shape of the building that counts, but what goes on *inside* the building.

If people think that new types of buildings are going to get all children over grade level in reading, forget it.

THE SCHOOL COUNSELOR AND CHILDREN'S AMBITIONS

For children who do poorly in school, routine visits to the counselor's office *can* be very helpful. It can show him that somebody cares.

Unfortunately, too many counselors don't act as the child's friend. Instead, they seem to feel that they should be giving the child psychotherapy. As if talking about your feelings toward your mother can change your reading level.

Counseling programs are growing all the time. Counselors do many things. Sometimes they spend a lot of time scheduling children's classes, an activity that youngsters used to be able to do with the help of a clerk. Other times, they do therapy. In some schools, children are sent to the counselor every time they misbehave, so counselors can become disciplinarians.

Counseling started as a way to help children decide what to do when they left school. By helping them with this, the counselor could help the student select those courses which would prepare them for this career.

Dr. Rothney of the University of Wisconsin did a follow-up on children who were counseled and those who were not. He found that there were few important differences between the two groups ten years after finishing school, and even fewer differences twenty years later.

This is really not very surprising. The findings in Project TALENT show that less than 20 percent of male high school seniors were planning the same career five years after finishing high school as they did when they were in high school. About one girl in four kept her plans constant, but this may be because some of them planned to go into homemaking at both points in time. Given the change in times, today's student is even less definite in his career plans than the student of ten years ago.

Luckily, youngsters who go on to college have much more time to make up their minds about what they want to do in the future. Four to six years can be spent deciding. If their parents have money, a year in Europe can help.

Only the poor are stuck with making up their minds while they are young. And since they have benefited least from education, they have the least information about the choices open to them.

We feel that a counselor should be a friend who takes an interest in the child that nobody else is interested in. They should also be teachers, giving the children information about the opportunities, agencies, and learning experiences that are available to them.

But they cannot "cure" anyone of poor school achievement and should not try.

SHOULD A CHILD DROP OUT OF SCHOOL?

If a child is doing poorly in school, the argument about whether or not he drops out becomes more a question of what is most practical than a question of his learning.

If a child is doing poorly in school, and is over the legal drop-out age (usually 16), there is not much that he will learn if he sits around another year or two. Certainly, he will not learn enough to make spending that time worth while. It will also be difficult to talk him into staying if he is flunking courses which will make him stay in school longer than other youngsters in his grade.

Drs. Kohlberg and Mayer of Harvard studied this problem and state, "In terms of future job success, high school drop-outs do as well as graduates who do not attend college; high school graduates with poor achievement scores and grades do as well as those with good scores; and college graduates with poor grades do as well as those with good grades. . . . There is no direct evidence that poor schooling as measured by years and achievement scores will increase their life adjustment or success."

In fact, there is some research which could be seen as encouraging drop-outs. In one, a group of ghetto youngsters received all kinds of encouragement to finish school. When they did, they found that the main source of jobs for black youngsters in their town, assembly line workers, had been grabbed off by kids who had dropped out during the last year. In another study, a group of men in their early twenties was located. The drop-outs were actually doing better in jobs than those with the same average I.Q. who went on to finish high school. After all, the drop-outs were more experienced on the job.

If a youngster is doing poorly in school, telling him to stay on probably does him no good. However, it might be well to suggest to him that he find his job *before* dropping out. There is nothing harder than to be between two worlds — the student's world and the worker's world — and belong to neither.

When he grows up some more, he may go for his G.E.D., a high school diploma that can be gotten by taking a test.

If the youngster is doing fairly well in school, he should be encouraged to stay on as long as possible. Even if he can start college, he may be a little more able to get a job than a high school graduate. If he gets an A.A. (two year) degree, he may get a better job yet. We're not saying this is fair, but that's the way it is.

Possibly, it is time to face facts. One of the main reasons for encouraging children to stay in school longer is the state of the technological society. With five or six percent of our population unemployed, and perhaps another five percent having dropped out of the labor market because of their inability to find meaningful work, school is the only way that we as a society can keep children off the labor market and supervise them at the same time. The morality of using schools for this end requires much more discussion and debate than has occurred.

SHOULD ALL CHILDREN GO TO COLLEGE?

Not too long ago, we saw an ad put out by an insurance company. It showed a shovel stuck in dirt and the message went something like this: "Is this what you want for your children?" The rest of the ad went on to tell you to save for college. Evidently, better a poor college student than a good ditch-digger.

The funny thing is that we can think of a lot of college trained job holders who contribute less to society than do ditch-diggers. Nobody panics when a teacher goes out on strike for a week, except then the parents are stuck with the kids all day which can be pretty rough. But let the garbage men strike and real fear hits.

Actually, the push for higher education is quite a new thing. It was only a little over 100 years ago that Massachusetts made education compulsory, and it wasn't until 1918 that all states had reached that status. In 1900, only ten percent of the 14 to 17-year-old group were in school, and only three percent graduated from high school. In 1941, fifty percent of the population completed less than ninth grade education. In those days, if you didn't do well in school you went to work in the mines, on the farm, or at the pushcart. At the beginning of World War II, five percent of the children graduated from college, and yet not only did they win the war, but began the greatest spurt in technological improvement ever seen in history.

We are not anti-education. But we try to be realistic. Setting up college as the goal for everybody is very cruel; that is, until colleges change their educational programs. Some children are good in school and some aren't. But when children get to school, almost all of the work is aimed at getting them to read, so that they can learn in text books in grades four and on. High school is a farm team for college, with the idea that youngsters who take academic subjects are getting ready for college, instead of schools being worried whether they learn or not. As a society, we spend half as much on post-high school training as we do on the twelve years of education that come before. If they get to college, it may be because they were forced. A recent Carnegie Commission found one in six college students attending against his will.

Getting into college usually means that the youngster has shown good enough skills in reading and language. No one cares if he has any other talents, whether or not he finds happiness in life, or if he will be a leader of men. In addition, you have to be able to afford to go to college. Many poor but talented students know early in life that going to college is out of the question. Not only don't any of their friends go, but they know that if they get a job they can help support their family. On the other side of the coin, we have a quote from Prince Philip of England, talking to students, who said: "I am one of those stupid bums that never went to a university — and a fat lot of harm it did me."

Of every hundred children, our overcrowded colleges admit only 45 of the seniors graduating from high school. Of those 45, only 15 graduate. The net result is that 55 percent of the children in high school who do not have the talents required to enter college are informed by society that they are academic failures.

Since only one in three of those who enter college ever graduate, these other two must be failures, too. Is it sane to call 85 percent of youth failures? Actually, it is insane. The stress on those college students who have academic trouble will be so great, that about four times more students who dropped out had looked for psychiatric care than did undergraduates in general, according to a Harvard study.

That may be true, you will say, but how will he get a job if he doesn't go to college? Unfortunately, many companies seem to think that if a youngster can sit through school till graduation, he will make a better worker. What is really true is that he may *get* the job, but in many jobs the amount of education completed by an employee has nothing to do with how well he does the job. As a matter of fact, Ivar Berg found some interesting sidelights to his studies which show that the amount of schooling has little to do with success on the job. Teachers are victims of the craze for college. They are forced by their contracts to go back to school almost every summer so that they can sit through the same old, tired education courses. They do this instead of working on their teaching. After getting enough graduate credits, the teachers want to leave teaching.

So it's not what a child learns in school that is important, but whether he finishes or not. And even this is changing. A recent estimate of 1971's liberal arts and education graduates showed that perhaps 40 percent are unemployed or underemployed.

If our society would not set values like that, we would all be a lot better off. What we really have to do is get realistic about jobs. White collar workers make more than blue collar workers and the gap is widening. What our society seems to say is that white collar jobs are for good people and people who work with their hands are dumb.

Most jobs do not need college training. Law, medicine, and psychology could all be taught on the job. What college does is separate the "right" people from the masses.

The question can be raised as to whether a child who does better in school is *better* than other children or merely different. Of course, society *makes* them better by valuing academic talents more highly than nonacademic talents. But even this praise of the scholar within our society becomes a fraud as the youngsters with good "school" talents, once out of school, finds that financial success is not solely determined by academic success. In fact, business tends to be run by people who have bachelor's degrees and who had "C" grades in getting there. Despite the fact that students of the social sciences typically have the highest average I.Q.'s in the graduate school of any university, we find that Ph.D.'s in these areas earn approximately one third of what medical school graduates earn. On the other hand, we find children who are seen as retarded in the classroom, but when they leave school, can often buy and sell many academically successful people because of their better ability to adapt to the world around them.

Despite the fact that many good students do poorly in the real world, the school ignores the child who can survive by his wits or nonacademic skills but does not have good literacy and language skills. This has led a President's Committee to the concept of the "six-hour retarded child" who is poor in school but "may be exceptionally adaptive to the situation and community in which he lives."

College should be for people who enjoy academic work. But it is very overvalued in our society. Children who do not do well in school should *not* see themselves as dumb or as failures! School smarts are just one kind of smarts.

Parents and teachers have to begin to "accentuate the positive," as the old song goes. They must deal with a child's strengths, not only with his weaknesses.

We must teach children to be proud of themselves and what they are. If parents and teachers can convince a child that he is a worthwhile human being, they have done all they can really do. Instead of more colleges, what are needed are more humane schools and more realistic requirements for getting jobs.

VOCATIONAL EDUCATION

When we were of school age, New York City had a string of vocational schools. Sound advanced? It was advanced in theory, but little advanced in actuality. New York vocational schools are where the "dum-dums" went, children who were not good in academic, language based skills, and who were sent off to vocational schools without much consideration of what other talents they might have.

These kids knew, their parents knew, and their teachers knew that the kids in vocational schools were dummies. Because society values language skills so much higher than nonlanguage skills (to show how such feelings are stated, the author of *The Emerging Republican Majority*, Kevin Phillips of the U.S. Justice Department, is quoted concerning the poor: "I don't believe in education for most people. Teach them how to use a lathe and let it go at that."), these schools became kind of a holding action, to keep the kids in school, to keep them off the streets, to keep them out of the labor market, and to keep them quiet.

But the youngsters did *not* keep quiet. First, they found that the vocational education was largely make-work with little relevance to the real world. Second, they found that no matter how well they did in school, the good jobs were often snatched for

union apprenticeship by kids who knew someone or were related to someone in the union, regardless of talent.

Then they ran into the "credentials barrier." S. M. Miller, of
N.Y.U., puts it this way: "We have a new guild system of credentials, licenses, certificates — largely built on the base of education
—which keeps people out of many occupational channels."

So vocational education did not work. Youngsters who would
rather work with their hands knew that academic work was the
best way to improve themselves. Vice-President Agnew expressed
concern in a speech that the U.S. is educating too many "opinion
makers who can't do anything with their hands" while it should
be training brick layers and carpenters. But he knew where real
value lies. As the Vice-President told an African leader, "it is
important to have the right kind of education . . . if this is carried
to an extreme, college graduates with doctor's degrees could earn
less money than carpenters."

U.S. Commissioner of Education, James Allen, recognized the
dangers of this kind of thinking. In a speech to the National Association of Secondary School Principals in early 1970, he stated:

> One of the most serious flaws in our educational system has
> been its ironclad separation of academic and vocational preparation.
>   . . . in addition to the damaging pedagogical and economic
> effects of the separation of academic and vocational education, there
> are even more deeply harmful psychological and social effects. Such
> separation tends to foster a kind of elitism, to formalize and accept
> — indeed encourage — a materialistic classification of 'privileged' and
> 'disadvantaged.' . . . With compensatory and remedial programs to
> fall back on for those who are not well served by our primarily
> academically oriented secondary schools, it becomes easier and easier
> to rationalize a public school system designed to prepare a relatively
> few people for conventional higher education.

Our feeling is that we can no more ask 14- or 15-year-olds
to make a decision on what they want to do in life than we can
ask college freshmen to pick their major and expect them to
stick to it. It has been seen in practice that attempts to do this
work with neither group.

We feel that two things are needed:

1. Vocational and academic education should not be separated, at least until near the end of high school. If we can decide

what it is we want our children to learn in school (see p. 107), we can then find ways of *how* to teach it to them. We do not feel that school should teach *some* children how to be a carpenter, but should teach *all* children how to use tools. Once they are done with high school, students with good language skills can go on for higher academic work while those who want to enter blue collar or service occupations (sales, retailing, restaurant work, etc.) can enter those programs. But why should the schools take on the job of training people for these jobs? Schools can teach *all* children what is involved in academic, service, and labor types of jobs and let the kids make up their own minds. But let colleges, factories, stores, etc., train their own people. Each of these jobs is too specific to train someone for anyway. Can we train a youngster how to be a salesman in school, when being a salesman includes selling stocks and bonds and selling used cars? A part-time two year course in school can be taught on the job in a much shorter period of time. Only by letting the group who will provide the job do the training will the training be relevant anyway.

2. A change in attitudes is necessary. People must be taught to value a person for what he is and what he does, not what degrees he has. Recently, in Scandinavia, there was a strike by professionals because they felt that the blue collar workers were getting too close to them in terms of wages. As long as we think of people who are better in academic tasks as *better,* instead of *different,* we are in trouble. Both academic and nonacademic skills are needed to make man rich and healthy. We have to begin to look at people in terms of how well they do, without calling what they do better or worse than what the next man does.

This is not to say that vocational education is without merit. Certainly, there are many occupations for which vocational training is necessary. Car mechanics, hair dressers, electricians are some that quickly come to mind. These skills are taught in vocational schools and are often necessary for employment. In many places, these courses are taught after graduation from high school, while in others they are taught as part of high school. Recent figures show that 16 percent of teenagers were unemployed, but that only five percent of those with vocational training could not find jobs. Furthermore, 85 percent of those who complete high school with vocational training find jobs in the field in which they were trained.

But, again, it was the vocational school which got these youngsters the job, rather than assuring that they would do well on it.

HOW ABOUT FREE SCHOOLS?

One should not have read too much of this book without realizing that we're not really turned on by schools. Schools spend more time teaching children how to conform than how to think. In order to do this, schools are kind of benevolent prisons (and sometimes not so benevolent), where the rules come first. Like prisons, so much time is spent on the rules that everybody forgets what they are *supposed* to be doing there, which is learning.

Over the past few years, many middle and upper class parents have realized that their children are just not Ph.D. material. Rather than accepting these kids as they are, or pressuring the schools to give these youngsters a more realistic education, they looked for excuses.

These parents decided that *their* children are creative geniuses who are being broken by the nonsense of the regular school. They (correctly) reasoned that their kids want to learn and (incorrectly) would learn if they could do their own thing.

So they started Free Schools. Instead of the lock-step of the regular school, they allowed the Free School so much freedom that, for most children, it was like turning them loose in an amusement park with a fist full of money. Some kids couldn't stand the great number of choices and so they did nothing. Some sampled a little of everything but never really tried any one thing. A few actually learned.

We feel that, again, somewhere between these two extremes lies the truth. First of all, you cannot take children who have been forbidden for six or more years in school to think, and expect them to move right into the Free School atmosphere. Secondly, in *any* school, a teacher *can* be a person who channels the students, interests, who keeps the student out of blind alleys or wheel-spinning activities, who can give some direction or choice to the student as to what to do next once they have found something that can turn them on, who can be a kindly friend to their pupils, and who can build in the reward of success in a learning experience.

Instead, Free Schools often find themselves in the place of the teacher saying to the student, "What do you want to do today, Martie?" and the student saying, "I don't know. What do you want to do, Angie?" We have seen children of high school age who know nothing of how their city is run, and actually majoring in yoga or some other type of cultural enrichment which may be fun but might better be taught elsewhere.

We have our own ideas of what schools should be like (see pp. 102-115). On the other hand, Free Schools probably can't *hurt* a kid and at least keeps many of them from the failure of regular schools. Most of them are a lot more comfortable for the children than the regular schools, which is enough to make us hope that this type of school becomes more popular.

But parents should not expect miracles. For most kids, putting them in a Free School is not the same as a brain transplant and will not get them a graduate degree in an Ivy League School.

Realize that it is often a cop-out. But given the alternative, regular school, cop-out you must in many cases.

Obviously, since we have been demonstrating up to this point that all children are different, we must conclude that the more options available, the better. Within any school, various degrees of structure are necessary. For some children, a high degree of structure is necessary. They want to know exactly what is expected of them, how, when, and where. Other children need a total lack of structure, in order to pursue their creative bent. And most children fall somewhere in between.

RESEARCH ON NEW EDUCATIONAL TECHNIQUES

In the excellent review in his book, *The Process of Education,* Stephens summarizes much of the research concerning educational programs by stating, "The constancy of the school's accomplishment is one of those things that everybody knows. It is part of the folklore that, in educational investigations, one method turns out to be as good as another and that promising innovations produce about as much growth as the procedures they supplant, but no more." Stephens reviews studies ranging from 1897 through 1953 which are consistent with Nachman and Opochinsky's statement that "Reviews of teaching research have consistently concluded that different teaching procedures produce little or no difference in the amount of knowledge gained by the students."

Stephens compared the research on team teaching, new math vs. old math, experienced teacher vs. inexperienced teacher, giving weekly quizzes vs. one exam a semester, independent study vs. "lock-step," small vs. large classes, the use of programmed instruction, and instruction by T.V. vs. regular lectures. In a few studies the children getting the new technique do better, in about the same number the children in the old way do better, and in most there is no difference.

In evaluating educational techniques, you have to take into account certain things. One is the *Hawthorne Effect.* This effect is well accepted because whenever you do something new, *whatever* it is, the performance of students or workers will usually go up briefly. Put music in an office, and production will go up for awhile. Pretty soon it drops down to where it was. Then you have to find something else new while figuring out how to get rid of the music without production dropping, because the workers like the music and will get angry if it is removed. So it is with schools. Many new techniques look good because of the Hawthorne Effect, but if you look at the effect of the new technique over time it is usually found to be zilch.

Another factor we have to consider is how committed the school administration is to make sure that their new techniques are proven successful. For example, if a school commits itself to purchasing expensive equipment, such as computerized typewriters which cost tens of thousands of dollars each, it may be too late to discuss whether they work or not.

Another problem is that one must look in the professional literature to find out what seems to work. But the editors of professional journals must be considered. Many educational researchers probably realize that it is much easier to obtain acceptance for a submitted research paper if the magic words "significant difference occurred . . . ." appear instead of "no significant differences were obtained." It has been rumored that many editors believe that, if significant differences (higher scores) in favor of the new procedure are obtained, this implies better research planning than if no significant differences are found. We once received a letter of rejection from a professional journal which said that the lack of significant differences in this study would probably not be of interest to readers and, furthermore, the results were not surprising since we had questioned whether any differences would be found.

There is probably no way to estimate at this time what proportion of research studies go completely unreported because their outcomes would be harmful to the researcher's career. Does the university professor teaching techniques of behavior modification, wish to popularize the studies which show that these techniques do not work? And, more important, if he did a small-scale study which yielded negative outcomes, would he wish to publish it in a journal which is widely read by others in his field? It is doubtful that there are many among us who are willing to state publicly that we are holding back the whole truth. It would be difficult for an assistant professor to publicly admit that psychotherapy does not work, speech therapy does not work, or remedial reading does not work. This would be directly threatening to the persons whose academic empires have been built on teaching how to do psychotherapy, how to do speech therapy, and how to teach remedial reading.

But, more important, is the fact that new educational techniques are usually designed to raise the child's scores on traditional achievement tests. To think — we spend millions or billions a year in order to get all children to score a couple of points higher on the Iowa or Stanford tests.

Again, we must raise the question of "What are we trying to teach anyway?"

CHAPTER V

SOME RECOMMENDATIONS FOR CURRICULUM CHANGE

WHAT ARE THE GOALS OF EDUCATION?

IN 1642, the Massachusetts legislature passed a law that all children must be taught to read. Five years later, they passed the "Old Deluder Satan Act." This act pointed out that Satan was trying to keep men from reading the scriptures. Every town of 50 homes or more was to provide a teacher, so children could be kept away from the influences of Satan. Looking around today, it looks like old Satan may be winning, reading or no reading.

Since the beginning of recorded history, the content of education has changed little. In Kramer's book on Sumer, we find the following quote on the content of Sumerian education by a student 4000 years ago:

> I recited my tablet, ate my lunch, prepared my (new) tablet, wrote it, finished it; then they assigned me my oral work, and in the afternoon they assigned me my written work.

Recent estimates are that reading and writing (reading put down on paper) account for as much as 90 percent of the success in a school curriculum. What is the purpose of this reading?

Going through textbooks on curriculum we find those which tend to be politically liberal talk in general terms. Purposes of education include teaching children the following: (1) Social values, such as the democratic way of life, patriotism, belief in God, belief in freedom, and the fostering of morality; (2) Individual values, such as the ability to think and make wise decisions, elimination of prejudice, fostering happiness, and human dignity; (3) Maintenance of the culture, such as in scientific and technological advancement, public health, citizenship, and learning about the roots of the culture.

More conservative educators talk of more specific goals. They want children to learn how to improve the technology of the culture and to prepare themselves for further education through the improvement of their basic skills.

Some critics question whether any part of any of these goals are being met. In *Culture Against Man,* Henry says, "The function of education has never been to free the mind and spirit of man but to bind them. . . . Throughout most of his historic course, *Homo Sapiens* has wanted from his children acquiescence, not originality. . . . The function of education is to prevent the truly creative intellect from getting out of hand." Littell says,

> . . . the public educational programs are overwhelmingly committed to technology and violence, and the representative product of the system is the technically competent barbarian.

Are these critics correct? Let us look at some sad examples. There would probably be little disagreement among educators that the schools should at least be teaching children about their rights as citizens. In *Parade* magazine of October 5, 1969, we find the following:

> At a base in West Germany 252 U.S. soldiers were read a sentence that came from one of the great political documents of U.S. history, the Declaration of Independence. They were told merely to sign the statement if they agreed with it, not to sign if they didn't.
>
> Seventy-three percent refused to sign.
>
> The Berkshire County High School student union conducted a similar experiment in Pittsfield, Mass. The group circulated the First Amendment to the U.S. Constitution, explaining that they intended to submit it to Congress as a petition.
>
> The First Amendment, of course, guarantees to all U. S. citizens freedom of religion, speech, press, peaceable assembly and the right "to petition the government for a redress of grievances."
>
> Of 1154 persons polled, only 4 percent recognized the First Amendment; 42 percent, however, agreed with the statement, 35 percent disagreed, and 23 percent refused to commit themselves.

The National Assessment of Educational Progress did a citizenship survey. The *Phi Delta Kappa* magazine summarized the results:

> One of the major findings is that a large percentage of the nation's school-age youngsters and young adults don't understand or value basic constitutional rights.
>
> The least understood or valued right, the citizenship survey reveals, is the freedom to express controversial or unpopular opinions. When asked whether three controversial statements about religion, politics, and race should be allowed on radio or TV, 94% of the 13-year-olds, 78% of the 17-year-olds and 68% of the adults believed they should be banned.

Such findings are dramatic because they show that many people are learning in school, but are not being educated.

Whenever we lecture a group of teachers or school administrators, we always ask them "What are you trying to teach anyway?" We do not accept such answers as "reading" or "to score well on achievement tests." Our question deals with the *content* of education. So much time and effort is spent on improving ways to teach children that the *what* to teach is forgotten. We feel that this is why education fails. More people are concerned with pushing new, popular, and expensive programs designed to do the same old thing, only better.

This leads to experimental programs. In education, the word experimental is often used to mean "novel" or even "bizarre." The things that go to make up good, strict research, such as good samples, controls and follow-up are often forgotten. In ten years, expenditures for education in this country went from 400 million to 4 billion dollars, often for new ways of doing the same old thing.

This money is aimed at getting children to do the same old thing quicker and better. But despite spending all of this money, it is doubtful that today's children learn more in school than they did 20 years ago. There is no question that they know more today, but that is because of television, and not because of school.

So we always ask educators to go back to their schools and ask, "What are we trying to teach anyway?" When most educators realize that they have no idea of *why* they are doing what they do every day, maybe they will sit down and figure out new and better things to do.

HOW CAN TEACHER EDUCATION BE IMPROVED?

We recently had an interview with the principal of one of those large eastern high schools that have so much difficulty. We asked him whether teacher's college prepared teachers for his school. He felt that they were pretty well prepared in theoretical matters, but in methodology — how to teach — they were not. We only mention this because this answer was a little more optimistic than we expected.

Most teachers have to go through four or five years of college but during that time, the only *real* information they get about how to teach is gotten during the several weeks of practice teaching. Here, an experienced teacher shows the student teacher how to teach. But, too often, since the teaching teacher learned everything she does on the job, it becomes a matter of both of them teaching in the same way they were taught as kids. This makes most of the time spent in school pretty much a waste.

We have some suggestions on how to improve this situation:

1. Even after becoming a teacher, most schools make their staff go back to the University during the summer. If they do not pass a certain number of credits every so many years, no pay raise for them.

In the March 1969 issue of *Trans-Action,* Professor Ivar Berg wrote of his findings in studying this. He found that, after getting enough credits in summer school, teachers often leave the schools for jobs that pay more for more education. "The school districts are, in a sense, encouraging the teachers not to teach," he wrote.

This seems to be a foolish approach. First of all, this system may push some good teachers out of teaching. Second, why should a teacher get credit for having a strong backside and tolerance for college courses that teach very little?

It would seem to make more sense if a teacher spent her summers improving her teaching. There are a couple of ways in which this could be done. A group of, let us say, fourth grade teachers get together during the summer and develop new materials or a new unit for their classes. This would bring the teacher actively into the curriculum-building business, instead of their having to depend on the textbook publisher's *Teachers' Guide.* Or else, an individual teacher could take on a field of individual study to incorporate what she learned into her curriculum. A teacher could, let us say, read three or four books on black culture and select out readings to put in different places in her sixth grade history course. In either approach, the teacher would be more deserving of a pay raise than by the make-work method of sitting in college classes.

2. One of the main problems in teachers' colleges, as in most professional schools, is that those who can, do, while those who can't, teach. The professor of education may have gone through school, taught a couple of years, went back for his Ph.D., and then on to be a professor. He is now in the nice position of not dirtying his hands on kids anymore.

We feel that anyone who teaches in college should, from time to time, be required to go back and *do* what he is teaching about. If he is teaching elementary education, he should go back and teach for one semester every three or four years. If he teaches administration, he should switch jobs with a school principal for a semester once in a while. This might force them into making college curriculums more in line with the real world of the classroom.

HOW DO WE FEEL THAT CHILDREN SHOULD LEARN?

In the American educational system, in order to learn, a child must read. If a child does not learn easily through *literacy* (the ability to read), he does not get educated. There is this single narrow gate through which we try to crowd all children. If the child reads well, he is in good shape. If he reads poorly, he can neither read his text nor write his test. Instead of using the thousands of words that this child can speak and understand, we try to teach him by means of the few words he can read. Does this make sense?

There is no question that we should continue to teach reading in schools. Reading is very valuable and we should try to raise each child's reading level as high as we can. But we also try to teach children math, music, art, physical sports, etc. In no case but reading do we tell a child that he must do well in that subject or he will not be allowed to learn.

For those children who read well (above grade level), reading is a very efficient way of learning. For the more than half of children for whom reading is difficult, something else must be found. Certainly these children should be educated *while* they are being taught to read.

We know from earlier sections of this book that remedial reading will not make a good reader out of a poor reader in most cases. We also know that most people read as little as they can once they are out of school. Is it sensible to put all of our educational eggs into the reading basket?

Why shouldn't we use the technology that we have on hand to educate children? Look at what we have:

Tape recorders for poor writers to take notes or for good readers to read the books into. In this way the poor reader can *listen* to a text.

Books on records are available for the blind. Why shouldn't they be used for the word-blind?

Films can put movement into what a text can only describe.

Videotape recorders, especially portable ones, are now very cheap. They can be used to make tapes which can be used over and over again or be edited when new information becomes available. Some school districts are already using them. If one class puts on a play, it can be shown to other classes. Guest speakers on one subject can be shown every year or in different schools. The number of field trips can be cut down. For instance, a tape of a city council meeting shot by one child can be shown to all children in several grades.

Entire classes can be recorded for children who are sick at home.

Science experiments can be taped and watched by the child alone and in his own time. Language classes have also been taped. Television shows can be taped and incorporated into the curriculum at an appropriate time.

Projectors can show a series of still pictures to children.

Art can be used for learning. A child can learn more about architecture or animals by trying to draw some buildings or animals than he can by reading about them, if he has this kind of talent.

Music has been used to pass culture on from one generation to another since the beginning of history. Can we learn more about British Imperialism in the 18th or 19th century by reading about it, or by listening to the Clancy Brothers sing about it?

Role playing is used to train all kinds of people. In graduate school we all role play. We play grown-up psychologist, physician, lawyer, etc., so that we learn how to really do it when we are great big professionals. Why not use more of it to teach children about the congressional system and socialism, instead of dry words?

Field trips mean more than taking a kid to the zoo. It means observing their city government in action, in watching how animals are slaughtered, and taking pictures of the local power company polluting the river.

Guest lectures are more available than most teachers think. Many companies, stores, and government agencies have people willing and able to come to school and tell the children about computers, retailing, and bureaucracy.

Discussion between children is seldom used effectively. Sometimes we think that kids can learn more from each other than they can from the teacher.

We call this "the bookless curriculum." Most schools have audio-visual libraries, field trips scheduled, guest lecturers coming in, etc. But they are seldom used in a *structured* way. We show a film one day, maybe a film-strip the next week, etc. Textbooks are organized, with one thing leading to another, with goals, and with outside learning experiences and discussion questions suggested to the teacher in the teachers' guide to that text. But no one has packaged a nonprint curriculum in the same way.

According to *Educational Technology* (February 15, 1968), "During 1966, schools and universities invested more money in films and audio-visual operations than any other group. Total expenditures for all segments of the audio-visual market were $961 million, an increase of $212 million, or 29 percent more than the previous year." In addition, regular classroom movie productions reached an estimated 1,500 titles while, also during 1966, there were an estimated 3,020 U.S. productions utilizing 8 mm. silent films made for schools. We suspect much more is spent now. Despite all of this money there have been very few efforts to really incorporate audio-visual techniques into regular school curricula. These films, as well as other media which can be used in classroom such as tapes, continuous loop projectors, records, language laboratory techniques, etc., have not yielded dramatic results because they have been used in an unstructured and oftentimes haphazard manner (called the "hangover curriculum" by one wag — "I have a hangover, I show a film"). Furthermore, just as there can be poor textbooks, there can be poor audio-visual materials.

The beautiful thing about most parts of the bookless curriculum is that it can be done alone by the pupil. If he has a learning center available, where individual cubby holes are available, he can plug in his tape recorder or phonograph, check out his film or video-tape, and do his learning at his leisure. The teacher is then released to truly become a resource person. The child can relax more, can work in groups, and generally enjoy education more. This is not a cop-out for the teacher. The teacher now has to actually *teach!* No longer standing at the front of the room, rambling on to students, she must now truly learn her subject matter so she can direct her pupils to new learning experiences or help them understand what they are just learning. Think of the possibilities!

This problem was recognized more than sixty years ago. In his 1908 text, Huey described John Dewey's concern about the

fetich of reading (in) that the first three years of school are to be given largely to reading and little number work. This traditional place was given to reading in an early century, when the child had not the present environment of art gallery, music, and industrial development, but when reading was the main means of rising and was the only key to culture. Reading has maintained this traditional place in the face of changed social, industrial and intellectual conditions which make the problem wholly different.

Both Huey and Dewey agree that it might be best for a child's mental development if reading instruction was eliminated — or at least significantly reduced in elementary grades.

If Dewey can be viewed as the father of the bookless curriculum, Marshall McLuhan may be the godfather. He possibly predicted the advent of the bookless curriculum by stating that "once a new technology comes into a social milieu, it cannot cease to permeate that milieu until every institution is saturated."

A bookless — or multimedia — curriculum has never been seriously evaluated. Classrooms are not usually built to handle such a program. The textbook is still king in the classroom. And yet there is much evidence that we are ignoring other ways of learning.

Research shows that the greatest amount of learning that takes place in life is during the first five years. During that time, a child usually learns to speak, to understand speech, and to live within his environment. He learns through touching, tasting, biting, rolling around, listening, smelling, watching, playing, and engaging in all kinds of other learning experiences. Suddenly, at age five, the child comes to school where he must be quiet and sit still. Thus after he has spent five or six years learning through all of his senses, suddenly attention is focused on one method — reading — as the principal means of acquiring knowledge. This is true whether or not the child is physiologically ready to read, whether or not the child speaks standard English, and whether or not his learning to read well will ever stand him in much good stead.

In order to really have bookless programs, there has to be agreement that children *can* learn in other ways. If schools would agree to this, major publishing houses would have packaged bookless programs ready in a year or two. Just because a child *does* read well does not mean that many parts of his program should not be bookless as well. Then, *all* children could get reading instruction that worked on their reading alone, without as much anxiety about failure for both the teacher and pupil.

We have used this approach in individual cases. For certain children with severe reading and/or writing problems who we saw in clinical practice, an individualized bookless program has been set up. In addition to a willingness to experiment on the part of teachers and administrators, local services for the blind have been found to be a valuable source of materials.

The critical question is, given the failure of remedial reading, are educators going to continue to spend all this energy on bringing to the many a colonial education designed for the few, or are we going to change the methods of education so that they are consistent with our technological age?

AN EXAMPLE OF ALTERNATIVES IN CURRICULUM

Now that we have discussed the "how" of teaching, let us talk of the "what." We are not setting this forth to be a guide to schools or parent groups. Instead, we would like to give an example of a curriculum in the hope that our example is far out enough that others will be able to sit down with a fresh look at "what are we trying to teach anyway?" We figure that we should try to get parents and educators to start planning curriculum all over again from the beginning, ignoring the bad experiences of the past, but rather starting from scratch. There is no question that other groups will be able to come up with plans a lot better than ours. But first they have to decide to start all over.

What we did was to sit down and say, "O.K., what do we want our children to know about by the time they finish elementary school?" By limiting it in age range this way, we avoided trying to plan for the secondary school, which is traditionally more flexible and more able to do these things.

Our thinking about this led us to plan our curriculum around the theme of "Individual Differences." By the time we were finished, it became obvious that what we wanted to teach children in first grade could be taught to them for six grades. Each of the units we outlined could be repeated cyclically during each year of elementary school experience, beginning with simple material within that unit at first grade and making the information more and more complex throughout each grade, while building on what was learned earlier.

This type of program would be very appropriate for bookless learning. While children were taught the mechanical skills of reading, and the emotionalism surrounding this was reduced because reading would be only one area of learning, the children could learn. Initially it would require a great deal of flexibility and experimenting to get the materials into an integrated whole, but it could be done. The next section covers the subjects we think could be taught. Let us look at one unit and speculate *how* to do it.

Several of the units we outlined deal with differences between people. Under the unit "Physical Differences" we included height, weight, skin color, hair color, hair texture, sex and facial features. A film designed for the first grade could emphasize differences in height and weight of children to point out that all children *are* different physically. Supplementary arithmetic material could be introduced by the teacher to train children in the concepts of quantitative differences. This would include the units of measuring height and weight and the concept that we do measure differences. As the materials on physical differences become more and more complex through the grades, we could introduce the concepts of adding and substracting, amount and distances, and multiplying.

You will note that the possibilities are almost limitless in terms of the types of materials that could be used. In the example given above, "Physical Differences," audio-visuals in first grade could be designed to point out that there *are* differences between people. As we went up the chronological age scale, more and more details could be brought in to repeat the fact that there are differences between *all* people and that these differences are expected and natural. Children could be taught that these differences are quantitative rather than qualitative. For example, within the area of skin color, it could be noted that the average hue of skin is actually a light brown, when one considers all the peoples of the world. It could be pointed out to children that white skin is actually a point lower down on the scale of skin colors. In this way, we could demonstrate to the children that having more pigmentation is not a better condition, nor is it worse, than having less pigmentation — it is merely different. This would of course involve teaching them some elementary statistics.

Hopefully, the outcome of such a program would be an education for the child while he is learning to read. By sixth grade, the unit on "Physical Differences" could include educating the children in terms of physical education, as well as entering into some of the sociological types of information encountered in geography and social studies in the upper elementary grades. In addition, one could also tie up these differences with some of the historical concepts developed in other ways. In other words, the point of such a curriculum would be to integrate knowledge into a meaningful whole, rather than to present it in a fragmented presentation which depends more on rote memory than integration of concepts.

Again, it must be emphasized that this type of curriculum should not be lock-step. To illustrate, let us say that there are four cycles developed in the area of behavioral differences. In the next section, we talk of what happens in grade one, three, etc. But this is only done to illustrate the passing of time. Some children might go through all four cycles, while some, who have more trouble learning, might go through only the first two, and at a slower pace. All could spend six grades — or years — in school, but each would wind up learning something different. Teachers could allow a child to follow his own interests in one area while reducing the time spent in another area. But each would learn at his own speed and in his own way.

But the important thing is that both groups of children would have learned the same thing, with one group seen as getting extra enrichment information. It would no longer be a matter of learning or not learning something, but of how much a child learns to master.

Sample Curriculum

Where did we come from and where are we now?
- I. Geographical Overview
    - A. Our town and its people
    - B. Our state or province and its people
    - C. Our country and its people
    - D. Our continent and its people
    - E. Our planet and its people
    - F. Our universe

(These units could be developed over six grades, emphasizing first the geography of the universe, beginning with specific information familiar to the children and becoming more and more complex as we move into astronomy by the time the sixth grade is reached. History could be emphasized to give the children some background concerning their town, state or province, country, world and universe. Differences in culture, political systems and economic expansion would be the logical direction for this unit to go in secondary schools.)

II. Creatures on Earth
    A. Man
    B. Varieties of Animals
    C. Varieties of Plants
    D. Varieties of Other Structures (including such differences as can be found in snowflakes, types of minerals, etc.)

(The purpose of this unit would be to demonstrate the differences and varieties of forms of life on earth. Information in the early grades would concentrate on the fact that there are differences, while more and more scientific concepts defining these differences could be taught in succeeding grades until the fifth and sixth grades, which would specifically deal with differences in all types of creatures, from one-celled through man as a science curriculum.)

III. Ways People Learn
    A. Seeing
    B. Feeling
    C. Doing
    D. Listening
    E. Touching
    F. Smelling
    G. Reading
    H. Tasting
    I. Practicing

(The purpose of this section would be to provide more and more complex information about individual differences. One of the subtle outcomes of such a series of materials would be an appreciation of the fact that people do things differently and learn things differently, and that we should respect these differences. Of course, it is hoped that a teacher could develop discussion to the point that a sense of pride in their individuality could be fostered in each child.)

IV. Physical Differences
    A. Height
    B. Weight
    C. Sex
    D. Skin Color
    E. Hair Color
    F. Hair Texture
    G. Facial Features
    H. Other Physical Differences
    (Discussed in the text above)

V. Behavioral Differences
    A. Activity Level
    B. Attention
    C. Impulse Control
    D. Temperament
    E. Social Relations
(In the early grades, media materials should be devoted to pointing out to children that many of their behaviors are normal variations seen in a population. The purpose of this would be to reduce the feeling of "badness" encountered by many children whose behavior in these areas is somewhat outside of the norm. It might be worthwhile to consider that this unit would not be presented every year, but might be presented in grades one, three, five, and six. After teaching that there are differences in grade one, grade three might emphasize some maturational processes to demonstrate how children's behaviors change. The

curriculum in grades five and six could be actually a beginning psychology course, in which the types of behavioral differences are explored more minutely, while ways of measuring and appreciating these differences could be advanced.)

VI. Talents and Traits
   A. Sports and Other Physical Activities
   B. Crafts
   C. Music
   D. Art
   E. Listening
   F. Writing
   G. Reading
   H. Speech
   I. Arithmetic

(The purpose of this unit would be to demonstrate to children that there are individual differences and how these differences are manifested. It would also serve to provide a more integrated approach to why we study the different areas mentioned above and how these are utilized in the real world. Children could try their hands at activities representing each area. In the later grades, the focus of such a unit could be on providing some occupational information and making children more aware of the different occupations available and the types of specialties that go into creating each occupation.)

VII. Where and How We Live
   A. Location Differences (Geography)
   B. Type of Area (Urban, Suburban, Rural)
   C. Types of Homes (including homes not found in the immediate area, such as tepees or cliff-dwellings)
   D. Weather

(The content of this unit would be more specific than that presented in Unit II. In early grades, the focus could be on the child's individual world, specifically his area. Background could be given to demonstrate why this area developed as it did. As the information became more and more complex, scientific concepts could be introduced, such as means of building houses, how we measure and control weather, and how our style of living may be reflected by such things as history — both in the physical and political sense — as well as geography. The impact of technology on living styles would be covered here.

VIII. Customs and Beliefs
    A. Religions
    B. Dance
    C. Dress
    D. Food
    E. Holidays
    F. Health Practices
    G. Manners
    H. Toys
    I. Games
    J. Stories
    K. Language
    L. Music
    M. Art

(The purpose of this unit would be to demonstrate the differences and attempt to develop a sense of appreciation in the way other people live. It will be obvious that the type of presentation could become more and more complex in six grades, while supplementary materials could be developed by the teacher to illustrate the types of information presented in the instructional materials and to have the children actually attempt to develop new customs and/or beliefs so as to better understand the natural sequence of their development. Later, this background could be used to help understand why our culture developed as it did. Economic and political factors would be brought in from other units. The rights of citizens would be the natural outgrowth of this sequence.)

IX. Transportation
  A. Forms of Transportation
  B. Development and History of Transportation
  C. The Importance of Transportation
  (In early grades this would be pretty traditional. In the later grades this unit could begin to provide some background in the essentials of economics. The problem of markets could be tied up with transportation and the need for moving goods and services could be demonstrated.)

X. Relationships
  A. Family
  B. Friends
  C. Neighbors
  (The focus of such a unit would be on differences, as well as similarities. Differences in family structure throughout the world could be demonstrated; while in the earlier grades, the definition of what constitutes a family could be demonstrated. Customs dealing with friendships, such as illustrating casual relationships to the "blood" relationships of certain American Indian tribes, could be utilized to demonstrate variations in depth of feeling. In the later grades, some aspects of sex education could be involved in this unit.)

XI. Rules for Living and Why
  A. Home
  B. Work
  C. On the Street
  D. Government
  E. School
  (A subtle outcome of this unit could be to educate the teachers as to appropriate behavior in terms of

tolerance and acceptance of the children. In addition, the children could be trained to accept differences in other children and hopefully reduce some of the problems encountered among children who are placed in special programs in the school, and who, because they are different, encounter hostility from other children. Certain beginnings of political science could be brought into the governmental aspects of this unit, particularly in instructing the children about the Constitution and Declaration of Independence. In addition, portions of this unit could be combined with materials in unit I, parts A and B, so children could learn about the way their local government is run.)

CHAPTER VI

SOME COMMONLY ENCOUNTERED--BUT SELDOM DISCUSSED--HEALTH PROBLEMS

INTRODUCTION

IT IS not our intention to make this section into one of those do-it-yourself health care books. However, it is estimated by some that 90 to 95 percent of children's visits to a physician's office are for things that do not need treatment or at least do not need special knowledge. Unfortunately, many parents very often take their children to their family physician because the family physician's professional society tells the family to have a family physician and to take their children to him for everything from problems in swimming to dating advice.

We believe that a wise parent or teacher can handle many of his own problems. In this chapter, we are discussing *some* common problems which often require some long-term watching of the child before the parent either does something or decides to do nothing. By no means are *all* problems discussed, but rather the few problems mentioned were selected to illustrate some points about child rearing.

In this book we are suggesting that many times a "problem" will go away by itself with age. What is needed in these cases is understanding and patience, not a cure. It's kind of like a parent recently told us, "the way to get cured of a learning disability is to graduate from school."

In those cases where medical attention is needed, it always helps if you know what to be looking for beforehand. The problems discussed in this chapter are things that are tough to pick up medically. Most important, it is the *behavior* of the child which needs watching. This cannot be done in a five-minute office call, but a parent or teacher who knows what to look for can often provide the clues to aid the physician.

"HIGH-RISK" GROUPS OF CHILDREN

There are certain groups of children who have a better chance of having school learning and behavior problems than other children. This does not mean that *every* child in these groups will have problems. In fact, some of them will do very well. The only reason we are discussing these is that it sometimes helps to know that if a child had some of these problems earlier, it is probably wrong to blame the child, parents or teacher for his learning and behavior problems.

Almost any complication surrounding pregnancy or birth is known to raise the risk of later problems. This includes infections, hemorrhaging (especially early in pregnancy) or other major problems. There have been some drugs which, when taken early in pregnancy, have been related to some later, school-age, problems.

Complicated deliveries, including breech deliveries or precipitous births, may also be related to such problems. Children deprived of oxygen at birth often have problems, especially if it is for a long period of time. An umbilical cord wrapped around the neck is often the culprit. Labor lasting more than 20 hours and other difficult deliveries requiring instruments and heavy sedation of the mother may also be a factor.

Premature children, weighing under 5½ pounds at birth, are more typically found in groups of children with learning and behavior problems than otherwise would be expected.

One type of problem surrounding birth which we have seen often with children who are retarded or having behavior or other school learning problems is seldom discussed in professional books or articles. Sometimes, when a mother is beginning to deliver her baby at the hospital, and the physician is not there, the nurse will *hold back* the baby. Holding the mother's knees

together and sedating her are often used to do this. We are not
sure whether this is to avoid the legal liability of delivering a
baby without a physician in attendance, or a feeling of inad-
equacy on the part of the delivery room staff. But knowing as
we do that the unborn infant can be very fragile, this practice
of holding babies back seems to us to be barbaric. Research is
needed on how often it is done and exactly what the effects are.
In the meantime, every time it happens the parents should routinely sue the hospital. That would stop it soon enough.

For many years, for a number of questionable reasons, breast
feeding has been considered old-fashioned. Some reasons offered
by experts range from the desire of drug companies to sell formulae, bottles, nipples, etc., to a puritanical attitude toward the
mother's breast. Whatever the cause, breast feeding has dropped
tremendously over the years.

With the drop in the number of mothers who breast feed,
there has been an increase in cases of digestive upsets, colic,
spitting up, diarrhea, constipation, as well as allergies to cow's
milk and formulae. Mother's milk is the best for an infant. Breast
feeding is also the most convenient. (As one old sage put it, "It's
always there. It's always the right mixture. It's always warm.")
We have known working mothers who have successfully nursed
their babies with minor adjustments in their schedules.

Oftentimes, mothers have been discouraged from nursing
by medical personnel who find it too time-consuming to encour-
age and help the mother. Fortunately, a group of women known
as La Leche League are in most cities and voluntarily will aid
interested women in learning about breast feeding. It would be
a true shame for a mother to be discouraged from the natural,
healthful nursing of her child only to discover that the new infant
does not thrive on the man-made substitutes. Expensive bassi-
nettes, strollers, play pens, and other equipment will do less for
the baby in its first year of life than the fine nutrition provided
by the child's mother.

Other problems of infancy which can effect later learning
and behavior include allergic reactions in the respiratory tract,
such as croup, bronchitis, and pneumonia.

Some children have severe cases of childhood diseases, such as measles, mumps, etc., at an early age. These children may have after-effects which impair their normal growth and behavior. Children who have these diseases, particularly if accompanied by a high fever for a period of several days, may be considered "high-risk" children.

If a child has a health history which suggests high risk, it is unfair to blame either the parents or teacher if the child is slow in development, hyperactive, or has problems with coordination or reading.

HEAD INJURIES

Two of the more common causes for head injuries are falls and organized sports. Falls are very common in infancy, especially in the new style homes that have open stairways to the basement and concrete floors below so that the child can land on his feet and still fall and bang his head. As the child grows older and gets into contact sports with poorly fitting equipment, this becomes a common source of head injuries.

If the child is knocked unconscious, is incoherent, loses his memory, is unenergetic, is vomiting, is sufficiently wounded to require stitches, or seems changed in his behavior, get him to the emergency room at once. In any case, let him rest.

It is wise, however, not to let him sleep. A child, following a blow to the head, may fall into a deep sleep which may suggest very serious injury. The child should be watched carefully to be sure he is not behaving differently than usual. After the child has been examined and found to be uninjured, should his parents notice unusual fatigue, sluggish behavior or continuing headaches, another examination should be done immediately.

There seems to be a greater chance of poorly balanced, impulsive, or highly active children having head injuries from falls. Follow-up studies sometimes show that behavior or school learning is worse than average after a child has a severe head injury. However, we do not know if that is due to brain damage or if the child acted brain damaged *before* the fall and might have fallen because of his poor balance or impulse control.

The important thing is prevention. Enclose cellar stairways. If a child is very impulsive, try to restrain him in dangerous places and look for where the danger is in all places. If a child is going into contact sports (that is, if you can't keep him out) see that the equipment fits properly.

MIGRAINES AND HEADACHES

For many years, migraine headaches were seen and are still seen by many as a form of emotional difficulty. Some felt it was a result of neurotic tension, others saw it as an attempt to punish the parent, and still others viewed it as the result of hostility toward the world.

The brain works on electricity. Thinking or reacting is a result of electrical impulses in the brain. Sometimes, these impulses can get out of hand, like a short circuit in a machine. The electricity then discharges in bursts which, when in the right place and strong enough, are epileptic seizures.

There is good evidence now that migraine headaches are the result of a similar type of electrical discharge in the brain or what we call a seizure-like activity. If medication does not help, hypnosis by a qualified and trained psychologist or physician can help.

Some children will complain about their eyes hurting with a headache. This is not surprising, especially for children who do not read easily. It has been shown that many poor readers have poor coordination of their eyes, and it is a chore to track along a line of words. It takes much more effort than it appears just to move their eyes along a line. Some children have eye tremors when reading which cannot be seen without special equipment.

These are children who often lose their place, skipping words or lines, or repeating lines. A simple, but not accurate, test for the teacher to try is to hold a pencil about 18 inches from the child's eyes. Tell him to focus on the eraser and slowly move the pencil back and forth across his visual field and up and down. Have him keep his head still. See if his eyes jump around or move smoothly. Some children can compensate, and read well *even though* their eyes jump around. For the child whose eye coordination is poor *and* who reads poorly, some extra understanding is needed. Reading is hard for him physically, and he can use a few rests from reading rather than reading for long periods of time. The pain he complains about may be *real* pain. Imagine how hurt *you* would be if someone called you a goof-off and you really hurt. For that matter, imagine how hurt you would be if you *were* goofing-off and someone caught you at it.

In the past, teachers allowed young children to use a marker to keep their place on the page. This helped children with immature eye coordination. But this support was not allowed after some "magic" chronological age. The question is always "why?" For some people, a place marker, or finger pointing, will always be helpful. If it helps, let's let it be. Reading is a tool, not a ritual dance. If it works for a child, let him use it. After all, our key interest is having the child enjoy and use his skill in reading.

STOMACH ACHES

Old fashioned stomach aches can be due to many things: flu, appendicitis, eating too much candy, etc. Most parents and teachers know how to handle these. However, there is another kind of stomach ache we want to discuss here.

Some children can get stomach aches when under stress. Some of these are also due to seizure-like activity (discussed in the last section) which causes pain in the stomach. Sometimes these pains can be so severe as to cause vomiting, dizziness, and extreme fatigue.

You are not going to take the responsibility of assuming that these pains are caused by abdominal epilepsy. However, you should be aware that some children whose stomach aches seem to coincide with school activities, such as tests, are not necessarily trying to pull a fast one. If a child says that his stomach hurts when it is time to go to school, he should be given the benefit of the doubt unless you can medically *prove* otherwise.

Some children will complain of headaches or stomach aches and ask to go to the nurse's office. More often than not, these are children who are having problems in either learning or behavior.

Even if you think he *is* goofing off, what is wrong with a little rest for a kid who is under more stress than his parents or teachers would be willing to take? The nurse's office should be a rest stop where a kid can get away for a few minutes in a socially acceptable manner without feeling like he is being punished.

We remember one case of a child diagnosed as school phobic (an abnormal fear of attending school which is commonly seen as an emotional problem) because he kept throwing up. When we, in September, insisted that the child was emotionally sound and physically ill, all specialists involved felt that we lacked understanding of the home environment. The child died in December — not of school phobia but of a brain tumor.

This child and his family had been in psychotherapy for a year because of his "emotional" problems. Think of the misery and guilt suffered by that family! We are not suggesting that every child who has a stomach ache has a brain tumor, or even if a rare child has a brain tumor, that there is a good way of discovering it, but rather to illustrate the dangers of calling anything that isn't discovered in a medical examination an emotional problem.

EATING HABITS AND HYPOGLYCEMIA

True hypoglycemia is typically diagnosed as part of a routine physical examination — if the examination is complete (which most are not). However, many children show symptoms occasionally even though a lab test may not show it. It is due to a deficiency in blood glucose. Symptoms include crankiness, headaches, fatigue, and sometimes confusion.

Some children never get diagnosed because the symptoms go away as soon as they eat something. Since most parents know that a hungry child is a cranky child, their children are fed before a physical examination.

However, if a child's behavior breaks down in school or at certain times of the day, either just before lunch, just before dinner or an afternoon snack, or before going to bed, this can be suspected. In such cases, arrangements should be made for the child to have snacks at these critical times.

Children's eating habits differ. The home or school which has a "clean plate club" not only does not understand children, but typically is forcing the child into bad eating habits. Similarly, if children are not allowed to eat in school when they are hungry, we are increasing the chance of having unruly and cranky children.

The latest thinking among some scientists is that it is better for digestion to spread several smaller snacks through the day than have three meals. In addition, there seems to be no reason to force foods on children which they do not like to eat. All adults have their dislikes in food. Also, we can all remember some food (or drink) we developed a taste for when we got older.

There are many children (and adults) who have food allergies. Sometimes the individual will have a built-in dislike to the foods that are harmful to them. To insist that the child "try something" may trigger off a sensitivity which is far more troublesome than the so-called "finicky appetite." As the child matures, "wait-and-see" is the best position to take. Many a parent who griped that the child will never try any foods other than hot dogs and hamburgers will look back fondly on "the good old days" when, in adolescence, the child develops a taste for filet mignon and lobster tails.

Protein is protein. Just make sure the child's diet does not have too many carbohydrates. If he prefers hamburger to steak, count your blessings — with the price of steak what it is. Protein is protein.

In some poorly nourished children, a condition called *pica* is seen. (Pica is a word describing the eating of non-edible materials.) This condition is often related to poverty since money for a proper diet is not available. However, it can and does appear in other children. It is sometimes seen in children recovering from a severe illness. The most well known and, possibly, most dangerous form of pica, is the eating of lead-based paints from flaking walls and furniture. In this case, the child develops lead poisoning which causes permanent brain damage.

Vitamin deficiencies and nutritional imbalance can affect the growth and development of children. Although this is more frequent among poor children, it can also occur among more affluent people who are careless in meal planning.

Children who have had severe accidents, falls or burning may show signs of uneven growth and development, which can be reflected in their diet.

If children are allowed some choice in what and when they want to eat, the chances are they will remain as healthy as if adults set up guidelines for them. It also helps to kind of stack the cards: buy fresh fruits, meats, and vegetables instead of candy and popcorn, and the chances are the children will develop a taste for them. Following this advice might also reduce the weight problems of some adult readers. However, there is a good chance that a person's weight is more a matter of how he was built when born rather than how much he eats. Surely, we can put on or take off some weight but, in most people, their fatness has little to do with what they eat. Of course, a person who is fat needs energy to carry his bulk around, and you get energy by eating.

PINWORMS

About 90 percent of all children have pinworms at some time in their life. Some wits claim that the other 10 percent are lying. These are tiny, thread-like worms which range from one tenth of an inch to almost half an inch in length. They are passed between children by hand to mouth. Most commonly, they settle in the anus and, in girls, in the vaginal tract. They result usually in itching and are most troublesome at night.

However, other problems can arise from them, depending on the child. Some children have painful urination or hold their urine, while others can cry out at night. To illustrate some of the problems which can occur, and the damage that results from ignorance, we will describe three cases we have seen.

A little eight-year-old girl was in third grade and had been treated in a community mental health clinic for one year. She was originally brought to the clinic because she seemed to be masturbating openly. The parents watched her at home and the school officials watched her manipulating her vaginal area in such a way as to be interpreted as masturbatory behavior. She was then sent to the community mental health center where one year was spent in psychotherapy examining the relationships of this child to her parents.

One year later, she was still showing this behavior. She was brought in for a psychological examination because of her school problems other than the masturbatory behavior. It was noted that her behavior was quite normal for her age and that there did not appear to be any bizarre behavior. Since masturbation is rarely seen over extended periods of time in children of that age, except when they show other behaviors which may be possible early signs of later mental illness, it was felt that all other possibilities must be ruled out. We asked that the child be examined by her parents for pinworms. Her parents detected them and brought her to the family physician who found that her vaginal tract was heavily infested with pinworms. Normal treatment with pyrvinium pamoate eliminated any further masturbatory behavior.

A second little girl was ten years old when brought in for a psychological examination. The parents were concerned that this child was having seizures at night. The child was observed at night twitching and moving about. The youngster had been seen by a pediatric neurologist who could find no other signs of seizures. Our examination of the youngster found that she seemed to be quite normal. It was then recommended that the parents have her examined for pinworms. When the neurologist was informed of this, he ignored this advice and referred the little girl on to a psychiatric unit at a local hospital. After several visits to this unit, the girl was discharged since no problem could be found. Following this experience, the parents took the little girl to another physician and specifically requested information about pinworms. Again, the child was found to be infected with them and treatment resulted in an end to this behavior which was interpreted as seizures.

Such cases as the two described above are more dramatic

than most. Other cases have been seen where the effects of pin-worms were not as damaging to the behavior of the child but nevertheless should be considered. For example, in a little seven-year-old girl who was referred for overactivity, examination for pinworms again yielded positive results. The effects of pyrvinium pamoate were not as dramatic in this case, although it did reduce her activity level to some extent in the classroom.

Unfortunately, parents often have poor information about pinworms and believe that they are caused by "dirty" house-keeping and lack of bathing. Since parents feel this way, they see pinworms in their children as a bad reflection on their house-keeping abilities and their personal cleanliness. In some in-stances, parents would be more relieved if a diagnosis of emo-tional illness was made. Pinworms are ever-present and can resist the efforts of the most dedicated housewife.

It would therefore appear, particularly among girls, and especially among young children, that awareness of the behavior which accompanies pinworms — scratching, waking at night, irri-tability, nightmares, stomach aches, loss of appetite, changes in toilet habits, etc. — could lead to a lessening of the stress which sometimes occurs. The child troubled with pinworms often is a fatigued child because of the restlessness in sleep. In the first two cases described above, two children had very unhappy ex-periences while two families underwent the expense and guilt of self-examination, when all that was required was a simple piece of plastic tape and a microscope to end the problem. In most cases, an inspection by the parents during the night is sufficient.

The fact that the medicine is expensive, and that poor chil-dren are at least as likely as richer ones to be infected with these worms, also requires some consideration of the current treatment of the problem. Since pinworms are probably more often detected by aware parents than by physicians, attention should be paid to the following questions: (1) Should the medi-cine require a prescription? (2) Couldn't a cheaper means of distributing it be found? and (3) Shouldn't parents be better educated so that the onus surrounding the anus is reduced, and cures started much earlier?

BEDWETTING (ENURESIS)

Most children become dry at night between the ages of two and three, although there are some who are not dry by 10 or 12. Even those who train early will sometimes have an accident at night. In addition, when stress is placed on a child, he may go back to old ways and begin to wet again. (That is why they advise you never to take the bottom bunk in the army.)

All children will have daytime accidents until they are well into their school years. These usually happen when the child is having so much fun that he tries to "hold it in" too long and doesn't quite make it to the toilet in time, or when the child is laughing very hard.

Children who train late very often have other areas of immaturity as well, such as those described in the chapters on behavior and school learning. It is often seen as an emotional problem, as if children are wetting their bed deliberately to punish their mother.

More recent research shows that the basis of bedwetting is most probably physical. Children who bed wet are often slower in physical maturation than the average child. They are frequently found to be very sound sleepers. Sometimes the size of the bladder may be a factor. Occasionally the bed wetter may have a physical problem that needs correction and treatment. Interestingly, bed wetting appears to run in some families and at least one parent was usually a bed wetter in childhood.

There are some do's and some don't's in handling the child who bed wets which may be helpful:

DO'S

1. Do get a thorough physical examination for the child.
2. Do remember that the child does not enjoy bed wetting.
3. Do put a plastic cover on the child's mattress.
4. Do help the child understand that bed wetting is not bad or shameful.

DON'T'S

1. Don't physically punish or shame the child.
2. Don't act impatient or discouraged about bed wetting.
3. Don't travel without a plastic sheet.

Sometimes parents can keep the bed dry by waking a child during the night. Limiting the amount of fluids for a couple of hours before bedtime can be helpful with some children. There are some drugs which show promise (like imipramine) in helping control bed wetting in some children. Some children have been helped with electrical devices which trigger an alarm when bed wetting starts. The child then, hopefully, will awake and use the toilet. In general, the child will grow out of the problem by the time he reaches puberty.

Most important to the bed wetting child is his sense of self-esteem. A bed wetting child should be helped to realize that bed wetting is not evil, but is a human difference. The child should also be reassured that he will eventually grow out of the difficulty.

The most healthy environment for the bed wetter is warm, understanding parents, a plastic mattress cover and a convenient automatic washer and dryer.

LACK OF BOWEL CONTROL (ENCOPRESIS)

In facing both this problem, as well as enuresis, we should look for simple answers first. One case one of us saw can illustrate.

A boy was referred for psychological services because he was encopretic. He was soiling his pants in school quite often, and this was certainly making the children who sat around him almost as uncomfortable as he was. One of us was asked to see him to see if there was an "emotional disturbance" underlying this.

The evaluation was quite routine. Nothing unusual was found.

Then, reaching down into our psychological bag of tricks, a very rare approach to such problems was used. He was asked, "Why do you do B.M. in your pants instead of going to the toilet?"

His reply was that the teacher only let them go to the toilet in groups and everytime they did, Charlie beat him up in front of the other kids.

Rather than put up with this, he would try not to go until he could get to the toilet without Charlie. He was rarely able to accomplish this.

Encopresis is relatively rare in childhood. About 1½ percent of children aged seven to eight have this problem. Again we note that "apples don't fall far from trees" when we learn that about 15 percent of the fathers of encopretic children had the same problem as children. Unfortunately, some studies show that less than half the parents who have such children seek help. This may be part of what Dr. David Silber of the University of Iowa calls "the obvious bowel-consciousness in our society." He also found that a number of encopretic children were toilet trained by their grandmothers "whose personal experiences with toilet training occurred in an era of more aggressive practices."

If a child is not bowel trained by the age of four or five, a physician should be consulted to determine whether there is a physical problem which may be interfering with training. There is a strong possibility of a physical problem in many encopretic children.

A careful health history should be obtained from the parents. One of the encopretic children referred to us had been given laxatives by her mother for a period of two years. This home treatment was the basis of the child's problem. In some instances, surgery may be necessary to correct the problem.

In some instances, a child may appear encopretic in school only. This may tell us more about the classroom situation than about the child. There is some irony in the fact that parents spend so much time in toilet training children and taking pride in the child's ability to take care of this need independently. Then the child enters school where he is often required to lose this independence. In some instances, he is required to regulate his bowels and bladder to meet the teacher's convenience. Not all children can do this successfully. Many children are shy about asking the teacher's permission to go to the toilet. It would seem logical to allow children to go to the toilet when they want. Children handle their own toilet habits in their home and should be allowed to do so in school. Some children will, no doubt, leave the room just to escape the routine. This is hardly reason enough to schedule toilet time. It might be more logical for the teacher to try to find out why a child finds the classroom so trying. Accidents will continue to occur in the classroom where the child is not given independence in toilet habits.

As with enuresis, physical punishment and shaming children who are encopretic should be avoided. We know much less about encopresis than we do about enuresis. Partly this is because this problem is less frequently referred for help. There is also a possibility that it is a less common problem in childhood. In our clinical experience, some children have had their soiling experiences under conditions resembling seizures, and medications have been helpful. Since this pattern is known in enuresis, can encopresis be far behind?

THUMB SUCKING AND NAIL BITING

More girls suck their thumbs than do boys. About one out of three or four children suck their thumbs. It is very common during the first two years of life and then tapers off naturally until, at adolescence, only about one out of a hundred will still be sucking their thumbs.

About one of three children bite their nails after about the age of five, and more *start* this habit after age five until about 40 percent are biting their nails at puberty. It usually goes away during adolescence. Children who bite their nails often have a parent that bit his or her nails as a child. Thus, we can see it is possibly a familial trait, and may even be carried by the genes.

For some wierd reason, many psychologists and psychiatrists used to feel that nail biting and thumb sucking represented an emotional disturbance. Many teachers and parents have bought this. We have heard of parents or teachers bandaging a child's finger, and even tying an arm up. One mother we know put it directly: "Don't suck your thumb or I'll cut it off." This child stopped sucking her thumb. Her whole arm broke out in a rash instead.

Why all this fuss over a common habit that usually goes

away by itself? Our advice: ignore it unless the child is drawing blood. If you cannot ignore it, face it, it is your problem, not the child's.

MOTION-SICKNESS

Many children (about 20 percent) get car sick. Usually, their parents had a history of car sickness as children. Symptoms can range from dizziness to vomiting. For some children, keeping them occupied helps. For others, dramamine helps, although it often will make them sleepy. Typically, they eventually grow out of motion-sickness.

There are some authorities who claim there is a relationship between car sickness and suppression of vision in one eye. The child may not look like he has crossed eyes, but still he may not be using both eyes. In case of the straight-eyed car sick child, it might be helpful to have the child's vision evaluated.

If none of this works, and a child complains of feeling sick on the night before a long bus ride for a field trip, understand that he (or more probably, she) is embarrassed about getting sick in front of others. Either let him stay at home or school, or see that he gets there by car (where stops can be made when he starts feeling sick).

HEARING LOSS

Most children with an obvious hearing loss are discovered by their parents. At a young age somebody notices that the child does not seem to respond well to sound. Soon the parents start testing the child by softly calling his name, holding a watch behind his head, clapping hands behind the child, and other homemade common sense tests. If the child does not respond to these, the parents should take the child to an audiologist, or hearing specialist.

Some children have hearing losses which are less obvious. Sometimes the loss is just in a few frequencies so it doesn't affect all sounds. It would be interesting if we could study groups of children who respond differently to male and female teachers.

This difference in reaction to the male versus the female teachers is usually assumed to be an emotional response. However, there may be a possibility with some children that high pitched voices are in a hearing loss region for an individual child. The child may not follow the directions given by a female teacher, not because of hostility to the "mother figure," but because of an inability to hear the teacher's voice distinctly.

Some children can have normal hearing but, when they have a cold or have allergies, they lose some of their hearing. Infections in the ear can also cause a mild hearing loss or even a more severe one which is bad one day and better the next.

Most children get their hearing screened by nurses in school. All too often, the equipment they use is not working properly or the children are tested under poor conditions.

If a child does not seem to hear you, or hears you inconsistently, or mishears many sounds, it is best to get it checked out. Have the school nurse look in his ears to see if there is drainage. Ask him if he has a cold. If neither of these seems to be the case, have an audiological examination done.

Official government estimates show that, aside from deaf children, about three to five percent of children have hearing losses, half of which require special classroom arrangements. If a child is prone to them, the teacher must keep in mind that he might miss what is being said. Understanding can help.

There are two other things to be considered. Some children hear but do not comprehend language well, while others have problems in interpreting what they hear (see discussion of auditory discrimination, pp. 50-51).

All too often parents and teachers punish children who just "won't listen" and it can turn out they have punished the child for having a hearing loss.

Things to do to make it easier:

1. The teacher and parent should get a written or verbal report from the audiologist so that they better know what to do.
2. If a child has the loss in only one ear, seat him so that his good ear is toward the teacher and, as much as possible, toward the class so he can catch discussions.

3. The teacher should face the class as much as possible when talking so that her lips can be seen.
4. Do not shout. This only calls attention to the "problem" when there is no need to. Move near the child (ten feet or closer) and talk naturally.
5. Use other means of communication to help. Gestures are very helpful, especially when dealing with a group situation such as moving through the halls. It is much easier to gesture "this way" or "quieter" with your hand than shouting it.
6. If he has a hearing aid, check it and be sure he has an extra battery in school.
7. Do not assume he heard. If he disobeys, assume he misheard unless it becomes obvious that he is using his hearing loss to avoid painful classroom tasks. If he is using his hearing loss to avoid school work, you have more important things to worry about besides his hearing loss.

Parents can adapt these seven recommendations to the home very easily.

IS PHYSICAL EDUCATION FOR CHILDREN REALLY EDUCATIONAL?

People who know us might think that our writing on sports is like having W. C. Fields lecture to Alcoholics Anonymous. Although neither of us has developed a local reputation in sports — either as participants or spectators — as child psychologists we *are* concerned with children.

We tend to agree with Mark Twain who said, "Work consists of whatever a body is obliged to do, and play consists of whatever a body is not obliged to do." Unfortunately, in most community and school settings, sports turn out to be work and not play for children.

We would like to examine some common myths surrounding physical education for children.

Sports Build Strong Bodies

There is no question that physical exercise helps a child develop and stay healthy. It does not necessarily follow that contact sports and highly competitive games are good for a young child's physical well-being. On the contrary, there is evidence that brain damage, bone damage, and tissue damage may be the end result of some sports programs for young children.

Dr. Loren Leslie, president of Sister Kenny Institute, indicates that Osgood-Schlatter disease is the swollen knee often seen in 13- to 18-year-olds as a result of sandlot activities. Drs. Robey, Blyth, and Mueller at the University of North Carolina summarized data for the number of players injured in high school sports and found that, depending on the circumstances, between 20 percent and 55 percent of participants were injured at one time or another. From their sample, they extrapolated to estimate that about 650,000 injuries occur annually as a result of high school football alone. Despite the expense of high school athletics, there can be as many as four times more head injuries using one make of helmet rather than another.

Many of the injuries which occur at younger ages do not actually appear until the children are older. High risk activities include blocking or running the ball in football, pitching baseball, running in basketball, skiing, hockey, and, of course, boxing.

Typically, the young child is not physically ready for highly competitive sports which either emphasize body contact or emphasize stress upon certain portions of their body (for example, little children who pitch curve balls over long period of time in baseball games). Children can and do receive concussions or possibly even minimal brain damage from poorly fitting equipment and blows to the head.

There must be a less dangerous way to build a strong body than taking the chance of ruining some aspect of a child's living for life, just so that we can be proud of their athletic achievements. H. L. Mencken, the famous American critic, once said, "When A annoys or injures B on the pretense of improving B, A is a scoundrel."

Sports Build Character

Character is difficult to define and hard to describe. But whatever it may be, we know that it isn't a muscle that develops with physical exercise.

People who are accomplished in athletics show the same

differences in behavior, self-control, life style, and attitudes others as found in all walks of life.

Babe Ruth was a sports hero because he played baseball well and not because he was a paragon of virtue. To suggest that sports build character is as ridiculous as to suggest that eating Wheaties develops champions.

Why feed these kids the pap at school, home, and church about love, golden rules, and fair play? An ad in the July, 1971 *Harpers* told it like it *really* is. This ad, requesting tax-deductible funds for the U. S. Ski Team, put it this way:

> If you're a skier, sportsman, or spectator, you know how important it is to win. And if you happen to be an American, you know how important it is for your country to win.

Recent articles tell us that coaches use amphetamines (uppers) and steroids (drugs whose side effects are not totally known as yet, but can include death) in order to win. The uppers allow the kids to go beyond the limits of good sense in terms of how hard they go out for the win. Steroids put weight on athletes because, in most sports, weight makes right. Pain killers and tranquilizers are also rumored to be used by coaches in the name of victory.

When winning becomes the overwhelming goal in sports, the ideals which we purport to hold dear take a second place.

Sports Prepare Children for Adult Recreation

This might be, except that we often emphasize the wrong sports. Schools enhance baseball, football, hockey, track, and gymnastics. Except for the really rare child who is so skilled in sports that he enters into games as a means of earning a living, and the few who *almost* make it and continue to play games in their 20's (typically softball for barrels of beer), most of us tend to ignore these sports once we have left school.

It is interesting to note that the most popular sports for adults are those which do not involve as much size and strength as they do skill and concentration.

Except in a few rare cases, the games that adults play are largely ignored in our physical education of children. Golf, tennis, bicycle riding, hiking, bowling, handball, squash, paddleball, etc., are activities which we *could* maintain for the rest of our lives. However, when most children leave school, they have little, if any, familiarity with such games other than what they have sought out alone.

Let's face it, the sports we teach our children at young ages are the ones we wish them to perform in large colosseums before crowds of on-lookers who prefer to watch rather than do.

Competition is Good for Children

Some form of competition is natural to many children under certain circumstances. However, as children become more and more involved in organized athletics, they realize that the competition is not really fair.

How can we ask children to compete when we know that so many of the sports which are inflicted upon them depend upon body size for success, and that children have no more control over their body size than they do over their eye color?

Telling a child to "try harder" in sports in the hope of "making it" does no good when he is slight of build and realizes that it helps to be 6'13" or weigh 400 pounds in order to be considered a good athlete.

Although we leave a few positions in sports open for well-coordinated, medium-sized people, we totally eliminate small people from most sports and seriously restrict the types of things that medium-sized people can do in many sports.

One of the worst features of sports programs designed for children is the lack of consideration for individual differences. Children develop physically at different rates, are different in physical coordination, are different in competitiveness, and different in interests. However, we often act as if they were all equal and it is therefore only a matter of "trying harder" to be good.

By disregarding individual differences between children, physical education can become one more area of stress for children. Even physical fitness programs in school have become competitive, ranking children by points with the less mature or physically handicapped child placing at the bottom of the chart.

The child is not considered for his individual effort and achievement, but is compared in "fitness" to others.

Since there are so many areas in school in which many children fail, why allow their games to become another source of failure and diminished self-respect?

Kids Want Organized Sports

In the old days of the sandlot, rules and regulations were flexible, to say the least. The number of strikes allowed the batter often depended on the kids' sympathy and understanding of the poorest player. Rules could be broken to keep everyone playing and to "even up" the game. A kid could get mad, throw down the bat, and go home if he felt he had a good cause.

For years, children have learned to play games by watching older kids and picking up the games themselves. For those who were very good, they pursued the games on their own time to improve themselves.

Now, we have set up a farm team system which is down to children of five to six years of age.

This is not the idea of the youngsters. Children below the ages of 12 or 13 typically dislike such highly structured and organized activities. It is rather the needs of the fathers and mothers which they are attributing to the children.

For example, it is reputed that the best gang fight ever to take place in St. Paul took place among fathers during a Little League baseball game.

In the absence of any studies where someone actually asked children whether they *like* sports, and assuming an honest answer, one can only talk from their own experiences. It was amazing to hear the spontaneous comments from some people we know when we told them we were writing on this subject. Typical was one adult who told us that he hated Little League baseball, but his parents always made such a big thing about how much he liked it that he couldn't quit without hurting them.

Another time, we stood and watched a couple of beefy middle-aged men hit baseballs to eight- or nine-year-old children. Traditional comments accompanied their efforts: "Get the lead out," "C'mon, now hustle," "You'll never make it that way," etc. In our society we attempt to structure relationships between fathers and sons, even to the point of financially supporting "Big Brothers" if there is no father. Is this how a superior (in size, power, and authority) friend acts? This probably best exemplifies the generation gap. Adults who demand that children compete with adults set the child up for failure and invariably offend the child.

Sports are for Participation

One of the more frequently stated purposes of sports programs is to get children "involved." In more affluent neighborhoods, this may mean a form of healthy babysitting — a supervised period away from home that yields all the supposed benefits accrued from sports programs. For the poor, it may mean "getting them off the streets." A child cannot steal, use dope, riot or lounge in an unseemly way if he is involved in a community center sports program.

Let us say that these are beneficial outcomes and should be pursued. This takes money. Is money being spent for participatory sports? Let us take our city of St. Paul, Minnesota, as an example. During the middle 1950's, the city spent $2 million for a baseball field designed to attract a major league team. Another group across the river in Minneapolis built a second stadium in the suburb of Bloomington which eventually did house the baseball Twins and football Vikings. Two million dollars shot. Now there is talk of another $40 million for a domed football stadium in downtown Minneapolis for the Vikings. This new stadium would be about ten minutes' drive from the 60,000 seat stadium at the University of Minnesota. Meanwhile, for some strange reason, the city of St. Paul went ahead and built a 16,000 seat arena as a part of its civic center. (North Stars hockey and whatever pro basketball teams that barnstorm through also play in a big new arena in Bloomington.) Another $14 million shot.

Each new high school that is built naturally tacks on a stadium to handle baseball, football, and sometimes track. Thus, the cost of each new school is skyrocketed by a facility that will serve maybe 60 to 100 boys a year. In fact, we would bet that it is the rare school that gets more than 300 or 400 boys a year to even *go out* for these sports. In addition, a high school football coach in St. Paul earns about a $1,600 differential for coaching beyond his regular salary. An additional expense is the cost of the equipment.

Thus, we can see that a large part of our public monies are spent for stadia where we can *watch,* instead of do. How many neighborhood swimming pools, bike paths, handball courts, tennis courts, ice skating rinks, etc., could be built and maintained with the money spent in St. Paul and Minneapolis alone on places to *watch* sports?

And note the sexism. Except for an occasional female track team, how many women ever become involved in programs which take place in those stadia? Other than a few cheerleaders who are allowed to lead cheers for the boys, over one-half of the student body (girls) are excluded from use of these costly plants. In fact, in St. Paul schools, women coaches are included in the intramural program rather than being paid on a schedule, like the men.

Thus, one can conclude that most of our sports programs are, in fact, an elimination tourney to cull out the most interesting (to watch) athletes. Must we continue to emphasize sports which yield professional or semi-professional gladiators to entertain the immobile public and enrich the business communities under the guise of an educational program?

The Poor Can Use Sports to Improve their Lot

"Look at so-and-so," one hears. "If it hadn't been for sports, he'd still be a poor southern farm kid." We cannot validate this scientifically, but it seems to us we hear this most often about two types of athletes: the super-star who is making ridiculous amounts of money in porportion to what he contributes to society, and the minority athlete who should be grateful for being exploited.

However, most of our organized out-of-school sports are

designed for middle and upper-class youngsters, because the poor simply cannot afford to buy the necessary equipment. It is for this reason that professional basketball and boxing are over-represented by poor urban kids (minimum equipment and space needed) while football and baseball are popular with poor rural kids (minimum equipment and a hell of a lot of space needed). These kids do not ski, play tennis or golf, or dive, because the facilities are not available.

It has been well documented in other places that the number of poor kids who can utilize sports to improve their lot is in-finitessimally small. Aside from the handfull who make it into professional sports, sports turn out to be another area of exploitation for them. Most minority boys, for example, who are recruited to play varsity sports in college find, after their four years of eligibility has been used up, that they have been counseled into easy courses to maintain their eligibility. In order to graduate, at least an extra year of college is required in order to complete their requirements for a degree. Needless to say, they rarely can afford to stay around without their athletic scholarship (body rental?) to finish their degrees.

Some Alternatives

All the above is not to suggest we are opposed to physical education, team sports, or physical fitness. As with motherhood, apple pie, and the flag, no red-blooded American can afford to reject the concept of the sound body.

We are merely suggesting some alternatives to our present system.

First, it might be well for adults to learn to allow children freedom of choice and some independence in game playing. Our society seems to be obsessed with the idea that we can teach all children anything and that this should be done in an organized and structured way.

Most of what children learn is learned by themselves; most children grow despite us, rather than because of us. They even can show understanding and compassion in social relationships when left alone. Adults can supervise and protect, but hopefully from a distance.

It might seem more appropriate to change the focus from structured competitive sports to the type of sports that people can pursue for the rest of their lives and which are less dangerous to growing children.

But most important, we must attempt to minimize the unhappiness which can come to many children who are not good athletes as a result of enhancing the few who are good.

Sports must be relegated to its proper place, as a form of recreation, rather than as a life style.

The uncoordinated or disinterested should not be made to feel inferior, but should be allowed to feel that they can do their own thing. Our present preoccupation with spectacles in the name of sports are already turning off many children.

Rumors abound that new means of getting youth into the ball parks as spectators are necessary because so many of them just don't care anymore. Possibly, they would care more if sports had been more fun for them as participants.

We should also face the fact that a perfectly normal, wholesome, contributing human being can develop to adult life without ever having been interested or involved in a competitive sports program. Some very fine people do not enjoy and never will enjoy competitive athletics.

With some modifications of our athletic programs for children, we might even develop a generation of real sportsmen who believe that: "It matters not if you win or lose, but how you play the game."

CHAPTER VII

TYPES OF BEHAVIOR PROBLEMS

CHILDREN WITH SEVERE PROBLEMS

T HIS BOOK is aimed at the parent and teacher of the so-called normal child (normal from the point of view that they are not now institutionalized). Some children have problems much more severe than the ones we are talking about. Probably less than one percent of all children are so disturbed or retarded that they need such specialized care that they are put away. There are three types of children who, if it is too difficult or painful for the parents to care for them, are either put in institutions or homes where people are paid to care for them.

1. *The severely retarded.* This typically includes brain damaged children with I.Q.'s in the trainable range, even though we may not truly be able to train them in self-care activities. Such children are recognized early in life when they are very slow in learning to walk, talk, and other important activities.

2. *The behaviorally disturbed.* These children are also typically recognized as such before school age. Seldom, if ever, does one see children with *severe* problems in the school. At an early age, the disturbed child may rock, hit their heads, twirl in circles, mutilate themselves, wander off, hallucinate (see or hear things that are not there), ignore people, have uncontrollable rages, talk nonsense (true nonsense, such as making up their own language. Caution: this may normally be done by twins), etc.

3. *The misplaced.* This includes some tragic types of cases we have seen. Some illustrations:

— A deaf girl institutionalized as retarded, without ever having had an audiological examination.

— A naughty — but not crazy — boy put in a residential home by his psychiatrist (the home was not filled with tuition-paid clients, and the psychiatrist owned part of the home).

— An Indian child placed in a foster home because the welfare worker is a racist and does not think that Indians know how to take care of their own children.

— A child who had been disruptive in school and the school staff finally convinced the parents to institutionalize the child, not because the child was unmanageable (they had managed him for ten years in that district) but because the school was *tired* of dealing with him.

— a child institutionalized by a clinic where the parents finally went after clinic-hopping for years. This clinic was trying to build a good reputation in the community, so their philosophy became, "if you can't do something, do anything."

This last group — the misplaced — are the children that this section is more concerned about. The first two groups have been written about, often well and sometimes poorly. Too often, writers try to make the third group sound like the first two groups. This danger must be avoided.

JUVENILE DELINQUENCY

A recent study of teenagers in Flint, Michigan, found that there are "almost no nondelinquent adolescents." Martin Gold found that most crimes were done in groups, and that even when parents knew about it, there was little they could do. In 1966, Gerald Pine wrote an article called "The Affluent Delinquent." He showed that more than 90 percent of children admit to committing crimes.

The rate of delinquency in a given community is often related to the number of laws and ordinances the community has and the size and vigilance of the police force. For example, many communities have curfew laws. But these laws are not always enforced with equal vigor. If a community is very strict in enforcing the curfew law, the rate of juvenile delinquency will be higher in that community than in a community where the law is ignored.

Delinquency statistics tell us more about who was caught rather than who was involved in delinquent acts. The chance of a child being declared delinquent, appearing in court and being sent to an institution is much higher among the poor. Where parents can afford lawyers or have the time to speak for their child, the delinquency charge is often dismissed. Policemen do not feel comfortable arresting children whose fathers may be the mayor, judge, physician, etc. When delinquent acts do take place, they are often not reported in certain neighborhoods.

In a community with which we are familiar, a group of boys vandalized the local elementary school. They were caught in the act. The parents of these children volunteered to pay the damages and handle the discipline of the children personally. Not one child was charged with delinquency. In a neighboring community, children were also caught vandalizing a school. They appeared in juvenile court, were charged as delinquents and three of the five were sent to reform schools. The other two were turned over to the probation department. The crimes were identical. The difference was level of income and social class of the families involved.

Thus, delinquency means being caught. And all too often being caught means being poor. We have personally witnessed such events as police being called because a white middle class child committed a dangerous act but, after his father chewed the boy out, the police left. Three days later, on the same block, three black children wound up at the police station for a much less dangerous crime.

There is one rich suburb that we know of that has almost no reported crime. Sure — there's crime — but it doesn't get reported.

Generally, there are three types of crime:
1) Some children do wrong on purpose. This would include those types of children discussed on pp. 71-72, who get into trouble because their self-image is so low. Their failure in school is directly related to this. Their feeling is "Why not? There is not much else for a failure."
2) Some commit accidental crimes. Accidental crimes include those that get committed because a child does not know it is against

the law, or because of bad luck. Fewer girls get pregnant than have sexual relations. Getting pregnant means that she is caught, but having sexual relations while under age is rarely caught. Getting caught with marijuana is a crime, and happens *much* less often than kids blow pot. Some young men are charged with rape when their only crime was sexual relations with a girl under eighteen. If a twenty-one-year-old boy has a love affair with his seventeen-year-old girl friend, he may be in danger of increasing the crime rate by being charged with statutory rape.

In general, these are crimes without a victim and the amount of punishment will depend mostly on how strict the society feels about areas of moral behavior. Crimes of this type change with social change. What was a crime in the 1800's is not necessarily seen as crime today.

3) A third type are those who cannot help themselves. Some research on genes and brain structure has been zeroing in on these problems. Others cannot control their impulses, like in fire-setting or some sexual activities called perversions. An example of this type of crime would be the Texas college student who shot and killed about fifteen people, including his wife and his mother. Autopsy findings discovered a tumor in an area of the brain which plays a strong role in control of emotions. Fortunately for society, these crimes, although sensational, are rare.

In all of these cases, locking them up does no good. Some constructive outlet in their society must be found.

TRUANCY

Recently, we saw a 14-year-old boy who had just run away from the third "detention center" (children's jail) in which he had been placed. He had been locked up in one for over nine months. We have seen eight- and nine-year-old children who were actually *taken away* from their parents and placed in foster homes or juvenile homes. In all of these cases, the "crime" was the same: truancy. Society is doing the children the great favor of giving them an education. If the children do not accept this favor, we throw them in jail.

In most cases, children who truant from school are under a great deal of pressure. Either they cannot cut it scholastically or the school is leaning on them for their behavior. Rather than make any adaptations in their programs, the schools often act like it is a battle of wills and that they must break down this child's resistance to authority. Some children get more upset by a teacher's unrealistic demands than others. If the teachers were treated so cruelly they would quit. The children *can't* quit. So they run away.

If a child is rich and/or white, he is often then placed in an expensive residential school or in a special class for "emotionally disturbed" children. If he is poor, he is usually placed in a foster home or jail. In most cases, these children are *not* mentally ill. Usually they cannot read well or are hyperactive. Sometimes, their teachers publicly point out how lazy they are or how bad they are, and sometimes the teachers beat them. The school always complains first to the family and usually the family beats them.

In many cases, if the school would let up on them, these children would attend (although, in many of the cases we have seen, you might ask "Why?"). More probably, if school programs were made meaningful to them, they would go to school more willingly.

In any case, the punishment seldom fits the crime. Those cases where the child is taken from his family are hard to understand. Most lawyers can tell you of divorce cases where the home was truly bad, and yet the judge allowed the mother to keep the child. Why must we assume that the school's failure is the parent's fault? And even if it were, does tearing up the family help things?

Putting the child in jail is also particularly cruel. Many children learn in jail, but the wrong things. They learn from other children how to burglarize, strip cars, forge, etc. Jail is usually a waste of the taxpayers' money because it does not improve the child — just the opposite happens, in fact. Furthermore, it is dehumanizing. Instead of building more detention homes, we would probably do better to invest the money in free schools and street academies for such children.

SCHOOL CRIMES

The worst school crime children can commit is truancy (see pp. 145-146). They get locked up for this. About five percent of children in Minnesota institutions are there for truancy and the number would probably be higher if truancy was not combined with some other category, like "incorrigible," "runaway," or "other." These four categories comprise over 50 percent of juvenile incarcerations in the state.

More minor school crimes include smoking in school, running in the halls, chewing gum in class, talking in class, not having homework, having the wrong lock on the locker, not having a pass to go to the bathroom, leaving the building, swearing, calling a teacher by his first name, speaking out or in a loud voice, etc. These more minor crimes often mean winding up at the principal's office or even being expelled.

Let us look first at smoking in school. How hypocritical it is to first seduce children into smoking through advertisements, without telling them that nicotine is addictive to many children, and then to punish them for it. Particularly in high school, where children see themselves as adults, and try so hard to prove it, having a teacher's lounge with smoke pouring out of it doesn't help.

Prohibition in the 1930's and the drug laws today probably demonstrate that outlawing something may make it even more attractive. Among teenagers, smoking has long been seen more as something cool to do than something enjoyable to do. It seems to us that since earlier efforts to prevent people from smoking (including advertisements) have failed there must be some new directions in which to go. For example, we would suspect (but can't prove) that smoking might be cut down if a space in the school yard was set aside for smoking. It should not be too comfortable and should be separated by sex so as not to make it too attractive. Kids should be allowed out there whenever they want as long as they have parental permission and as long as they meet their responsibilities to be in class on time. After a few months of watching themselves being isolated from the main social activities, possibly the smokers could become involved in talking new smokers out of it. On the other hand, maybe nothing can work as long as the only argument being used against it is some tenuous evidence of cancer 30 or 40 years hence.

As far as the other "crimes" go, there are three main types. The first is due to the fact that we expect behavior from children which they cannot achieve. Whenever we speak before a teachers' group, we always notice that there are many who come late, some who chew gum or even eat while we are talking, many who whisper to each other, and many who complain about sitting still too long. However, the school's insistence that the children tolerate these bad conditions often pushes many children into the criminal class. The second group include those children whose culture is different than that recognized by the school and problems arise because of misunderstandings. Children from certain cultures, for example, quite normally use words seen as curse words by the school. The third group are those children who are poor students or nonconformists. These kids either are constitutionally unable to adjust to school or, due to the great pressures they are under and cannot deal with, get into trouble.

It is our contention that the third group would be reduced in size if schools took more account of the first two groups. If a child is having trouble with reading, the last thing in the world he needs is to be disciplined for chewing gum. It would not be so bad if he got the heat for chewing gum *instead* of his poor reading, but you, he, and we know that he will get heat for chewing gum *plus* his poor reading. As we are trying to point out throughout this book, the more you punish a child, the worse he will be. On one hand a child must take responsibility for what he does. On the other hand we adults must learn to overlook many of the child's weaknesses as we expect him to overlook ours.

This does *not* mean that children should not be held responsible for their acts. But responsibility must be defined realistically. Children have never met the expectations of parents. But, in school, there should be some leeway given so that the child feels a sense of responsibility if he completes something, instead of feeling like a weakling for having caved in under pressure.

DRESS CODES IN SCHOOL

There is an old saying, "You can't legislate morality." Throughout history, people who govern have tried to tell other people how to act and dress. In some cases they were quite successful, mainly because they had the power to hurt, torture, jail, or kill people who disobeyed. In this country's early history, many people were put in stocks, tarred and feathered, jailed, or burned at the stake because they were "different" (it might be added that these "different" people often owned a nice piece of land, and after burning them, by some coincidence the guy behind the persecution often got that land for a song).

Schools have long had dress codes. These are based on the idea that "nice people" dress in a certain way. Further, it is another way of demonstrating control over students. Many people forget that before World War II, many boys were sent home from school because they had a "Heinie," which is today's crew cut. How times change!

The more rules that are made in school, the tougher it is to enforce them. The only simple way of having a dress code is to do what is done in many private and parochial schools, that is, have the children wear uniforms. This is the only democratic way of doing it, because then all children look alike. Even here you might have some trouble, because some poor children could not afford to buy the uniforms.

We cannot give any particular advice on this because today's no-no can be tomorrow's high fashion. Think of the number of parents who screamed "Wear a bra!" to their teenage daughters only to see today's jet set braless.

The more relaxed a school administration is, the less trouble it will have. Some rules have to be made, but the fewer made the less trouble there will be in enforcing them. Besides, why should taxpayers put up $18,000 a year for an assistant principal to go around measuring the hem height from the floor? It may be fun for him, but kind of silly in the long run.

SCHOOL PHOBIA (FEAR OF GOING TO SCHOOL)

For some children, the idea of separating themselves from their home and going to kindergarten may be a terrifying experience. These children are frightened for many reasons. Remembering what they have heard about school from older kids in the neighborhood, they may be a little more dependent on their mothers than many kids, they are shy, or they may just get frightened more easily than other children. But when it comes time to leave for school they may cry, beg, claim they are sick, cling to their mother, throw up, have a tantrum, refuse to get out of bed and get dressed, and some other rather creative behaviors which seem to fit their needs.

Children tend to grow out of school phobia. Given everything else equal, there are probably fewer problems the second week than the first, fewer the third week than the second, etc. There are also probably fewer school phobic children in first grade than in kindergarten, fewer second graders than first graders, etc., given everything else equal. But not all things are equal:

1. If one teacher seems to get more of her share of school phobic children than others, the principal should keep a close watch on her. She may be mean or too demanding.

2. If the children start showing anxiety about food at home, find out what is going on in the lunchroom. Some supervisor or the other children may have started a "clean plate club" or some other pressure to get the child to eat what he does not like.

3. Sometimes children will be afraid because of a real situation. For example, we saw a great deal of anxiety in several young children in one school. The children would not tell why, but some skillful eavesdropping spotted the reason. The school patrol children, who were supposed to be helping these small children cross the street, were acting like a junior version of the Secret Police. This behavior is very interesting, because the behavior of the police patrol may reflect the tone of that school building. If you have a principal whose idea of order is to scream and bully, the children will take on those same values.

4. Another problem may be some bullying children either on the way to or from school. Like us, a child cannot get very turned on by the possibility of getting beat up on any given day. Some parents feel that it is "just growing up" to have this

happen. Nonsense. Most children grow up without having been bullied over a long period of time and do not seem to suffer by missing this privilege. The parents should contact the principal who should use his authority to stop the behavior. Neither the cruelty of the bully or the fear of the weaker boy is an emotion worth maintaining.

In cases of school phobia, it is important that the child attend school daily. Allowing the child to stay home can indicate to the child that he can succeed at this game.

It is very difficult for parents to stand firm in the face of a frightened, crying child. However, a firm, but warm, approach does work. Take the child by the hand, put him in the car (even if you have to borrow one), drive him to school, take him in the front door, drop his hand, turn around, and go home.* In some instances, it may be necessary to request help from the school principal or school nurse. If the child's fear is so overwhelming that the parent feels unable to bring the child to school, the principal or nurse can be requested to pick up the child and bring him to school. After a few days of being taken to school, the child's fear will probably let up. The most difficult times for the school phobic child are following a school holiday or a weekend when the symptoms may reappear.

Interestingly, the school phobic child is often a successful student. This type of child frequently is afraid of making mistakes and sets very high standards for himself.

Efforts should be made to try to get the child to develop a more relaxed attitude about himself and his school performance.

ANXIETY

Anxiety is a fear which is not *necessarily* related to a specific event. Fear of the dark, fear of going to school, are not fears

---

*During the first few days or even weeks of the early grades of school, the child may show anxiety and ask the parent to go to school with him. Once at the school, they can run in without looking back. If it is not inconvenient for the parent to do so, and if it does reduce the child's anxiety, why not? Like all things discussed in this book, anxiety is relative. Some children are more anxious than others by nature. The thing that is different about the school phobic child is that he *won't* go, instead of preferring not to go.

of specific consequences, such as "If I do this, that specific thing will happen to me." Rather, it's "I'm afraid something bad will happen but I don't know what."

Some children are born more sensitive to how people will react to them, or to how high they set their own standards of performance. However, most anxiety is based on some real fact. The child who does well in school may be afraid of going to class because he has seen and heard what happens to others who goof-up in class. He *knows* that one of these days he will do something wrong and the same thing will happen to him.

The more demands put on children, the more anxious they will probably get. Many children will learn to hide their anxieties by boasting, lying, or avoiding anxiety-producing situations. If a child gets beaten down enough, he may lose many of his anxieties because he starts setting very low standards for himself. This is seen in the child whose attitude seems to be, "I'm eventually going to get it for something I can't control anyway, so I might as well get it for something that is fun for me."

Ghetto children are particularly racked with anxiety. They *know* that they are being rejected by teachers, welfare workers, bosses, shopkeepers, bus drivers, etc.

Sometimes children with anxiety are called neurotic. Sometimes they set up rituals which last for a long time.* Most people will call behavior neurotic if it interferes with their life.

True neurosis just is not seen that often by the clinician. Too often if a child is showing his anxiety, he will be sent for some kind of psychotherapy. What professionals try to do here is make the child understand why he is anxious so as to make him less anxious. Often they (the professionals) feel that they are successful with such children because children grow out of some fears, and change their way of showing them over time.

---

*It is the length of time and the stage of life which is important here. All children go through some rituals like "don't step on the crack, you'll break your mother's back" or sleeping with a teddy bear. These are normal at a certain age and may last a few days or a few years. So what?

However, the best way of reducing anxiety is to remove the thing that makes them fearful. If they are afraid of the dark, put a small night light in their room. If they are afraid of school, make schools humane.

SHYNESS

Some children are born shy and will die shy. Some grow out of it. It often seems to be an *inherited trait*, which is to say that these children are that way because it runs in the family, and is not developed at home.

Because of this, it is ridiculous to try to make someone less shy. Telling them to "Speak Up!" is asking them to do something that is very painful for them. A shy child speaks softly and the teacher can help by placing this child at the back of the room so he can speak toward the rest of the class. This also helps because he knows who is looking at him while he speaks and what their reactions are. If he is seated near the front, all he knows is that there are eyes on his back. It can make one quite paranoid. Save the front seats for bold children.

One girl we know was so shy that she never volunteered to speak in class, speaking only when called on. For some reason, her teachers became very upset with this. The girl was an excellent student but traditionally schools have felt that it is a sign of interest or motivation for children to raise their hand and volunteer in class. We explained to the girl how silly this is, but in some teachers' classes it is a matter of survival to raise your hand. We recommended that this girl make an effort to raise her hand once a day, and once only. She did and her teacher was satisfied. The girl did not change, and probably did not contribute much to the class, but she *did* conform.

The parent or teacher who points out that a child blushes, no matter how good natured he is in pointing it out, will make that child dread the next time that he will be forced into a situation where he *knows* he will blush. Children who blush can spot a situation where they will blush a mile away. If a teacher allows a class to laugh about it, every time one of those children is called on in class, it will cause the same feeling of fear in that child as the parent or teacher will get if he has the feeling that he is about to be insulted by a head waiter.

COMPULSIVITY

The careful, neat child is usually a joy in the classroom. Typically he finishes his work and will stay with a job until it is done.

However, even this can be overdone. Some children show a strong *need for closure*. This means that they have a very strong need to complete whatever they start. The thing is that *they* decide in their own mind what is meant by completion. If you ask them to write lines of the letter "a" on a page, they may not truly feel finished until the entire page is full of a's. If you tell them to start a section in their workbook, it may be difficult to interrupt them even for something important.

Such children are often highly anxious because they feel that they have not achieved the level of completion they should. Often, they have some social problems in that their more freewheeling friends may find their behavior difficult to understand.

There is not much that need or should be done about this child besides understanding him. Giving assignments in small blocks of work helps because then they can finish, even though they may be anxious to get on with more. Whenever possible, avoid interrupting his work to ask him to do something else — this will make him anxious. As the child grows, we hope he can channel this carefulness into his studies or job, and be a success.

PERSONALITY TESTING

There are many tests which are called personality tests. The two which are most popular are:

A. *The Minnesota Multiphasic Inventory (MMPI)* is usually given as a paper and pencil test. It is useful as a *screening test*. This means that, if we did not know much about a group of people, this test could give us some idea as to who to look at more closely.

B. The *Rorschach* is the famous inkblot test. It is fun to give and fun to interpret. It does not usually tell you much about a person, though.

The thing about personality tests is that they rarely have to be given. If someone acts strange, you do not need a test to tell you that he is strange. Nor is there much reason to give such tests in school, especially without the parent's permission. Most children who act up in school do so because they do not fit into the academic program. To give them a test to see if they are "emotionally disturbed" is foolish. Wouldn't your emotions be disturbed if you had to sit someplace for six hours every day and couldn't do anything right?

WHAT CAN WE LEARN FROM A CHILD'S DESCRIPTION OF WHAT HE SEES IN A PICTURE?

Not much. Parents and teachers should be careful not to overinterpret pictures. We had a friend, a psychologist, who was called up to school to see his son's kindergarten teacher. Dramatically, she held up some of the boy's finger paintings. "What do you make of this?" she demanded. Fearful that his son was flunking finger painting (he was already a candidate for remedial cutting and pasting), he stammered, "I don't know, what do you make of it?"

Her eyes narrowed. "Look at these reds and blacks. There's rage and depression here." Then she looked at him suspiciously and said, "What's going on at home?"

Beating a hasty, stammering, apologetic retreat, our friend fled home and cornered his son. "Listen, you. Why don't you use other colors besides red and black in your painting? Can't you once in a while throw in a yellow or an orange?"

The boy looked at his father with the disgust of the philosopher looking at the peasant. "The light colors are on the other side of the table and I'm afraid I'll knock something over reaching for them. So, I use the colors on my side. What's wrong with that?"

THE BRAIN INJURED CHILD

Many of you have recently seen discussions of brain damaged children in the press. Both their behavior and school learning are blamed on their "minimal brain damage." It is reasoned that such children are out of control of their behavior because their brain was injured, either while in the womb, at birth, or after birth (malnutrition or disease can cause brain injury). There are many things which are blamed on minimal brain damage (neurological dysfunction, hyperkinetic syndrome, perceptual impairment, brain injury, or any of the other names pretty well reserved for the same thing). In fact, a government study found about 100 different areas of poor adjustment which were blamed on minimal brain injury.

Frank brain injury is usually seen as the result of a blow to the head. Minimal brain injury is usually seen as a group of symptoms or behaviors that we *assume* are caused by an injury to some of the systems in the brain but not all of them. Birth injuries, malnutrition, measles, blows to the head, high fevers, and other like problems can be blamed.

There are two problems in calling someone a minimally brain injured child. First, there is little agreement among professionals in defining brain injury. One professional may call a child brain injured, while a second professional may not. Part of this problem involves the number of symptoms that can be involved. Does it take one symptom? two? how many? and how bad must the child be in that area of behavior to call it a symptom?

A second problem involves age. *Every* symptom described in a minimally brain injured child occurs normally at some age. What is more active than a four-year-old? Where do we find less impulsive children than two-year-olds? Thus, it is not the behavior, but the age at which the behavior occurs which *makes* it a problem.

The idea of brain injury is a mixed blessing. On the negative side is the fact that it *can* be used as a cop-out. Many parents would rather call their children brain injured than slow in school.

On the other hand, it has led many parents and teachers to look at their children as organisms, instead of something that changes by merely trying harder. This leads to some special consideration, tolerance, special programs, and more acceptance.

The behaviors most typically seen in children called brain injured are hyperactivity, poor impulse control, short attention span, and distractibility. Each of these will be described in the following sections. The opposite kind of child may have as many or more problems as he grows up. The very slow moving, low energy, compulsive or persevering child is sometimes called *hypoactive,* also discussed in this chapter.

It is quite probable that the number of brain injured children goes up as society demands more and more conformity of children. The more a school demands of a child in academic excellence while sitting quietly and attentively in the chair, the more we have to find some reason why the children will not go along with this.

People often ask us if we will call a child "brain injured." We will call him anything if it gets people off his back.

We will discuss below the more common and important signs of brain functioning that can get a child into trouble.

HYPERACTIVITY

The most commonly recognized problem in the lower grades is the overactive child. Such a child can be a problem to the parents before school, and for him it helps to live in a climate where he can play outdoors and no one notices.

But when such a child, usually a boy, gets to school, he has problems. Traditionally, children sit still in class. For some reason, teachers feel that a child learns best if he is sitting still, has his hands clasped, and is looking straight ahead. This may not really be so, but the teacher is under pressure to maintain a quiet classroom. The teacher who allows children to move around, to interact with each other, to learn from each other, and to make noise as children do, is suspect. We know of one teacher who worked that way and children who had hated school in the past now could not wait to go. They spilled out into the halls in their learning and their room was full of laughter. This upset the other teachers around her, who had quiet rooms, and the principal fired her after one year.

Hyperactive children wander in the room, cannot sit still when they are in their seat, are in constant motion on the playground, cannot stay quiet, can be unpredictable in their affection (hugging adults or other children), can have temper tantrums, may be eneuretic (see pp. 127-128) or accident prone, and generally appear happy because of the ease with which they laugh. However, they are not happy because everyone leans on them.

Young children are very active. In the first three grades of school, there may be one to three children in a classroom of 30 who are so active as to interfere with their own learning and the learning of other children. Whether they will be called hyperactive or not depends upon the teacher's tolerance. There are usually no more than two or three primary grade children out of 100 who are such a problem that everyone agrees that they are a problem. The problem largely disappears in later grades. Very few children in the upper grades are truly hyperactive, although there are many children who, because they are not learning well, are disruptive in the class.

Most kindergarten teachers can spot a hyperactive child quite well. One good way of handling them in the school is to hold them back in kindergarten for two years. Since, as pointed out above, almost all children are hyperactive as preschoolers, it is obviously a question of delaying their school experience as long as possible. Maturity can take care of many children who are active in the lower grades.

More important is tolerance on the part of the parent and teacher. There is a very good chance that the hyperactive child's father was highly active as a child, too. The child will probably always be a little more active than most, although puberty may slow him down some. Some can put their hyperactivity to use as a grownup. We know a middle-aged man who *still* cannot sit still. However, he uses it for good advantage since he is a professional athlete and a nonstop businessman.

Many hyperactive children are given drugs to slow them down (discussed below). All too many children are given drugs. In one midwestern city, ten percent of all school children are on drugs to slow them down. This is terrible. No more than a few children in primary grades, and *very* few in upper grades, should get drugs because they are active.

The long run effects of drugs are not known. More hyperactive children tend to have parents who had difficulties in adjusting than do nonhyperactive children. Whether this is due to hyperactivity causing the problems, or hyperactivity leading to rejection by society which leads to problems, is unknown at this time.

We really cannot measure activity level very well. There are ways of doing it, but they are very expensive and may not be accurate enough. For this reason, children are usually classified as overactive, normal, or slow moving. In all probability, the activity level of children, if it were measureable, would again look like the normal curve (see pp. 16-21). However, before measuring, we should consider age. If we drew the normal curve of activity by age, second graders will be less active than first graders, although there will be *overlap* (some second graders will be *more* active than some first graders).

So again we face the problem of where to cut the curve so that we can call everyone abnormal who is below the point on the curve. If we expect children to sit like a bunch of robots, there will be many problem children. If we assume that many children can learn while they move around, and if we are a little bit more flexible about age and start some children in school later, many of the problems would disappear.

DISTRACTIBILITY

When children are too little to obey us or to know danger, the wise parent will often try to distract the child from what he is doing and get him interested in something that is less of a problem. This works well because small children are so easy to distract. Usually, we can distract them *visually* (showing them something bright or interesting), *auditorily* (making a sound that interests them), or *tactually* (touching them).

This can be a factor in older children, too. One day, one of us was called to a school to see the teacher of an "emotionally disturbed" boy. The teacher was met outside of her fifth grade room and she was asked exactly what was being done to make her believe that the boy was emotionally disturbed.

"Well," she explained, "he hides under his desk." Admitting that this was a little different, she was then asked what he did while under the desk. "That's the strangest part," she said, "he does his workbook under the desk." This we had to see.

Stepping into the room, it was plain to see where most of the problem lay. The room was, like most school rooms, a large rectangle. Across the ceiling, the teacher had hung four or five wires from side to side. On each wire, the teacher had hung little strips of red, blue, white, and green foil. As the breeze moved in the room, these little strips moved, reflecting the light. It almost looked like a dance hall with one of those multicolored reflectors which turn in the room.

It took throwing an arm over the eyes to get out of the room without going mad. Once out, we faced the teacher in the hall again. "Hmm," we said, being a professional, which suggests that one is thinking when he says "Hmm."

"It's your strings with those hunks of foil on them!" we cried triumphantly (one has so few triumphs in this business that every time you do, you find yourself crying triumphantly). "That child is well adjusted. Because he is constantly distracted by the foil waving in the wind, he goes under his desk where he can't see them. In this way, he can complete his workbook. Take down those strings with foil on them and your problem will disappear."

It would have been nice if this had been successful. Unfortunately, a P.T.A. meeting was coming up and any teacher who does not have all kinds of bright, gaudy displays in her room is thought to be goofing off. Most teachers are taught that their classrooms, especially in the primary grades, should be brightly decorated. Classrooms should *not* be brightly decorated, because the bright decorations, pictures, and maps distract the children from their learning tasks.

This one case wound up okay anyway. We got the teacher to put a screen up in one corner of the room behind which a seat was placed so this boy could do his seat-work without being visually distracted.

It helps to place a distractible child's desk facing toward a blank wall so that visual distractions are cut down. If he is distractible to sound, it is a tougher problem because classrooms are not very quiet. Even if the teacher has scared the other children into not talking, they are moving around, dropping pencils, etc.

One thing to try is to face the auditorily distractible child to the wall and let him spin around at each sound. He may quit just from fatigue. Recently it has been suggested that background music cuts down distractibility. Letting him sit out in the hall is another maneuver. It is very important to explain to the class that these seating arrangements are not a punishment, but a way of helping the child learn. The children will probably accept it. Children are much more able to accept individual differences than are adults.

But the important thing is, whatever works is good. Each child must be experimented with individually. Trying something out is the best way to find out if it works.

One caution must be made, however. The teacher or parent must be realistic in terms of their expectations for a child. If the teacher asks young children to sit still and quietly for any length of time, they *have* to get distractible. All too often, teachers equate a child's being quiet with their being ready to learn. Not too long ago, we visited a kindergarten and found all the children sitting quietly in a circle. Because they were quiet, the teacher felt they were learning. What they really were was frightened of the teacher, which contained their restlessness and distractibility. At that age, children seem to move around more naturally.

Traditionally, schools have over-valued long bouts of seat

work. This is particularly interesting in that, during a recent course we gave for teachers, their biggest complaint was having to sit still for two hours.

LACK OF IMPULSE CONTROL

Almost everyone who has had a child has had the experience of their child getting "wild." You take him out to visit someone with a child his own age and the two stand there and avoid looking at each other for a good hour while the parents squirm. Finally, when they do get up enough nerve to deal with each other, you start wishing they hadn't. One child stimulates the other who, now stimulated, stimulates back until both of them are one big bundle of uncontrollable impulses. Soon the parents are yelling to get the children under control. The parents want them under control, the kids want themselves under control, but it cannot be done until they are separated and can calm down. This behavior is called *impulsive,* and it is a natural thing for all children to lose control of their impulses sometimes. Impulsivity increases when the child is stimulated or fatigued. Adults who have ever been to a cocktail party should understand that we all lose control sometimes, even if it is an impulsive blurting out of a true opinion followed by the sickening feeling of "Oh, why did I say that?"

As we grow, we gain more control of our impulses. An infant is a live mass of impulsive behaviors, trying to do whatever he feels like doing right at that moment. The more our nervous system matures, the more we are able to gain control of our impulses, the more *socialized* we become.

Like everything else that depends on maturation, some children take longer than others to learn how to control their impulses. In the early grades of school, there are usually one or two youngsters who are lagging behind the others. The children are walking in a line down the hall, one bumps the second who turns and impulsively hits the first child.* Time, and keeping

---

*The question of guilt becomes important here in order to tell the difference between the child who strikes impulsively and the one that does it out of plain meanness. The impulsive child will not usually have planned it ahead and will

him out of situations where he will act impulsively, can work with this type of child.

What is usually done is to *structure* the impulsive child's situation as much as possible until he matures sufficiently to control the behavior. This means that the parents or teacher has to anticipate where problems can come up and try to head them off. He has to be kept out of situations where he will probably get in trouble. For example, if he tends to throw things on the playground, he has to be either kept away from the things he throws or the teacher must subtly let him know that she is nearby just before he would normally throw something. Often, placing a hand on his arm gently can remind him of the social realities, and he can control himself.

Impulsivity takes many forms in children and probably accounts for the most dangerous and difficult to control behaviors. There are some children who break their toys and furniture, fight, tell lies, and are reckless as young children. As they get older, they steal, vandalize, set fires and are cruel to other children and animals. Usually they are also hyperactive and have a history of some of the high risk conditions (pp. 117-119). The same drug treatment used for hyperactive children (pp. 157-159) is usually the most successful in dealing with lack of impulse control. However, if the child lacks impulse control without hyperactivity, we are not sure anything works except environmental manipulation. Such children usually are so frustrated by failure that they strike out.

HYPOACTIVITY

Most teachers love the quiet, slow moving child. Typically, he is in control of his impulses and not at all a behavior problem.

---

usually be truly sorry afterwards. But this is, in many children, the case only when very young. Being yelled at enough for impulsive behavior may lead some children to develop a defense against their constant guilt and develop a defiant self-justification for their behavior. But different actions have to be taken for the mean child who likes to hurt others. It might be worth while to talk to the parents and find out where he is learning this type of behavior. Young children are taught or are so frustrated they learn how to hurt.

Although some teachers may get concerned, he tends to be overlooked in most classes. He *may* have some problems if he is so slow moving that he does not get his work done. Then, in contrast to slowing down the hyperactive child, we may try to speed this one up.

As he grows older, he may lack the aggression to "get ahead." Instead he may be very content with his lot and wait for the world to come to him. Measuring such a child in our society, we may find that he is beaten out by the grown-up active child who is able to channel his energies into succeeding.

His lack of activity is due to a lack of energy. About all that can be done is a medical referral to see if there are physical problems which reduce his activity level.

CHAPTER VIII

ATTEMPTS TO CHANGE BEHAVIOR IN SCHOOL

WHERE CAN THE PARENT OR TEACHER GO FOR HELP?

THERE ARE usually three places that a child is sent because he has school learning or behavioral difficulties. The family or neighbors, the clinic or hospital, and the school.

The first, family or neighbors, is not usually helpful because there is too much emotion involved. Asking grandma for advice usually is not helpful because, bad as the child is, grandma knows that her child never had enough sense to raise children either. The same goes for well-meaning neighbors, where competition or plain old meddling can interfere.

Going to the mental health clinic or hospital is usually where the most is done *to* the child, but all too often not enough is done *for* the child. First of all, clinic or hospital people often just do not know what goes on at school. Certainly not in all cases, but in too many cases, professionals in their clinic focus on the family without even considering that almost one half of the waking time spent by the child is in school.

Typically, much time and effort is spent in diagnosis, and sometimes treatment is available for a relatively short time as well. One negative effect is, by sending a child to a mental health clinic, the child is immediately labeled a problem, whether he is or not. But in any case, it is the family and school which still have the responsibility for carrying the main part of the load.

If the problem never gets out of the school, or if the ball is passed back to the school, it is the school psychologist who must be held responsible for acting as the middle man between school, family, and other agencies. He is, therefore, probably the person to contact first.

We are not entirely satisfied with this set-up. We feel that the school psychologist has a very tough position, because he works for the school.

We feel that what the child needs in the school is his own advocate. More and more professionals are brought in to work with (or on) the child, but who speaks *for* the child?

Who will point out the myths which underlie so much of our educational thinking? Who will tell administrators and parents that, by definition, 50 percent of children *must* read at grade level or below? Who will tell school board members that education today, as it has always, depends almost exclusively on the child's having enough language and literacy skills to survive, and there is little available for children who have skills in other skill areas? Who will tell teachers that many nonconforming behaviors of children are due to lack of impulse control, and not because the mother works or the father doesn't take him fishing?

The school psychologist *should* be the person to use his good offices to speak on the child's behalf — so that demands are not made on children which are not realistic in terms of what we *know* about normal child development and behavior. The psychologist should try to get both school and parents to adjust in order to accept the child more as he is, to emphasize the child's strengths and de-emphasize his weaknesses. Unfortunately, our profession as well as our society is problem-oriented. The weaknesses of the child become the focus of attention, resulting in many ill-fated programs to "cure" the child of being himself.

Furthermore, the psychologist works for the school, is paid by the school, must maintain relationships with the school principals and teachers, and must depend on the teacher's confidence to give him referrals.

We feel that the best way of changing this is to no longer have the psychologist employed directly by the schools. Instead, there should be school psychology clinics. These should be supported by the schools but not run by the schools. Medical personnel and social workers (who work as the middle man between the family and community agency) could be attached part time to such a clinic. But only in this way can the psychologist work *for* the child, have follow-up contact with the school, and be used more efficiently.

Sometimes, to make a point, one overstates his case. This is not to say that many agencies and school psychologists are not helpful, understanding, and knowledgable advocates for children. Possibly, this section reflects our frustration in working with some people in the so-called "helping professions" who are so concerned with their own egos, professional behaviors, and loyalty to the institution for which they work, that they forget the needs of the child.

Perhaps the parent and teacher can help change this by approaching such professionals with the question of "What will you do to help this child?" instead of "What is wrong with this child?" Also, demanding as an end product some action instead of an extensive diagnosis full of jargon, which does nothing for the child, may help influence these professionals to switch their orientation. After all, all professionals must satisfy the people who refer to them, or they are out of business.

EVALUATING DISCIPLINE CODES

Every school has a set of rules that governs it. This covers such topics as what credentials are needed to go to the toilet, what style notebooks are used, how far away from the school a child has to be before he can smoke, what type of lock must be put on a locker, etc.

We recently spoke to a faculty of a school that was asking some real questions about their set of rules. They asked our advice on how to go over the rules to see if they are working. We suggested that they set up committees, each committee taking one set of the rules that the school had. In each committee, two people should be selected, either through volunteering or election.

The first person should be a students' advocate. As a matter of fact, it could be a student (or two students) who took this role. His job would be to protect their constitutional rights. He could question whether the school had a right to open a child's locker without permission, whether he could be questioned by a police officer* without the parents' permission, etc. In other words, he is the committee's conscience.

The other person's role is to ask "why?" For every rule, the committee should be able to answer why they have it, and the reason should be a little more practical than the fact that schools have always had that rule.

The goal of this procedure should be to eliminate as many useless rules as possible. One elementary school principal we know set a new school rule: Outside of the classroom there would be no more rules. The only exception was that if there was an infringement on someone else's person or property, the children involved and a faculty member would work it out. Little change was seen in the building. As many children ran in the halls as did when it was against the rules, but now they weren't getting into trouble. The children were allowed to move freely about the building which only seemed to increase their sense of responsibility. He felt that the best example of change was the time a girl came to him to ask if he couldn't reinstate the rule against gum chewing. It wasn't as much fun to chew gum anymore.

WHAT TO DO ABOUT CHEATING IN SCHOOL

Teachers become very upset when children cheat. Usually they tell the parents and everyone sees it as a crime, or at least that cheating today will lead to a life of crime.

---

*Many high schools now have "police-liaison" officers in the school. In some schools they are armed. We have heard of instances where they use kids as stoolies to squeal on others, where they question youngsters without permission, and where they shake down the youngsters in school. Not only that, the schools make official records available to them. We once checked the records of one of them and, based on his salary, it cost the taxpayers over $200 for every police-type contact (many of their officers' contacts were more like a social worker's). Often, these programs only enforce the image of school-as-a-jail to children.

The truth is that very few kids cheat on everything. Some will cheat on one thing, others on something else, but they *all* cheat sometime. Children who are aiming at goals which are hard to reach probably cheat more than those who do alright by themselves. Two examples of children who cheat a lot in school are the child who does poorly and gets chewed out for it, and the child who does well but is satisfied with nothing less than being the best.

Some cheating can be harmful while some types might even be helpful. The child who steals another's paper, thus hurting someone, is doing something harmful to another. But this is rare. Often, setting lower goals for children can reduce their cheating. Indicating to these children that you are satisfied with what they are doing may convince them that there is no need to cheat.

Some cheating can be used well. For example, we always get upset when a child copies from another's paper. Who is to say that this child will not learn as much by copying from that child's paper as he would have by copying the teacher's writing from the blackboard? We have never really considered that children may learn well from each other. In fact, children may learn better from each other than they learn from a teacher.

Maybe the problem of cheating would go away if we allowed children to work with each other more, and if we did not force them to compete with each other so much.

It is very doubtful that cheating has a harmful effect on the child. The problem is more that it bothers the teacher. Cheating or helping each other out is bad in itself because it is against our tradition of the puritan ethic. H. L. Mencken, the famous American critic, once defined puritanism as "the haunting fear that someone, somewhere, may be happy."

To really fully understand cheating in school, we must first try to understand children. When children come to school, they have no idea what grown-ups mean by cheating. Before school, very few children know what cheating means. If they know the word at all, it is something they have heard used in game playing. It is not used to describe helping each other. If a child helps another child to tie his shoes, it is not called cheating. If a child zips another child's jacket, it is not called cheating. Whenever a child helps another child, parents and others tell the child that they are good children. That is, until the child starts school. When the child enters school, he learns what cheating is. Cheating is helping each other with learning. It takes a long time for little children to really know what is wrong with helping each other in school.

Adults, such as parents and teachers, often forget how children learn from each other and, in school, see this helping as bad. They believe that if a child copies from someone else, he is doomed to a life of crime.

Cheating could be completely removed from the list of school problems if the attitudes within schools would change. Because schools place so much importance on children competing with each other, and spend so much time testing children, cheating results. Children who find the school work difficult will turn to other children for help. When grades are emphasized, many children will cheat for grades. The need to be best will lead many children to cheat. If competition is not important, if grades and test scores are not important, and if the child is not required to do tasks that are too difficult for him, cheating is no problem.

Schools are beginning to realize that children learn well working together in groups. Helping each other can be a good way for children to learn. When the school is a place where children can be relaxed and learn at their own rate without worrying about the standards set for them by others, cheating will no longer exist.

Now this does not mean that children should not be given strong values about the rights of others or helped to recognize property rights of others. Children can be aided in developing honesty and respect for others without feeling they are dishonest when they help other children or look for help from other children in school learning.

PARENTS AND TEACHERS WHO SHOUT

From what we can tell, most American and European peoples have treated their children pretty poorly for quite some time. Shouting at them and hitting them seems to be the way that parents have of dealing with their children. We find this discussed in stories and plays that go back quite a few centuries.

Not all people shout at and hit their children. Many Indian, African, and Oriental groups have built into their culture more of a tolerance for normal child behavior. Some of these so-called primitives feel that it is impolite to treat your children so badly while you are so polite to everyone else.

As times goes on, and financial problems have lessened in some European and American families, parents become less tense. They can deal with their children as people. They can resort to shouting in an emergency, but most of the time, some parents and children can converse with each other in the same way they converse with their friends. It might also be pointed out that parents who often shout at their children have children who often shout at each other and at their friends.

As the child grows up in the family, he comes to expect certain behaviors of his parents. Included is no shouting, some shouting, or a lot of shouting. But he learns to live with it, even though some children can *never* be comfortable while their parents are shouting. However, it is usually only the parents and other adults who raise him that shout at him. In our culture, most other adults treat him quite nicely. Visitors who come to the home gush over him when he is small, pat him on the head as he gets bigger, and are indulgent when he gets ready for school.

But then he gets to school and finds a new breed of adult. Many teachers treat their children like a bunch of recruits in the old army. The teacher will often shout at her children with very little reason. Most children get very upset by this (see discussion of school phobia, pp. 149-151). Children quickly learn to hide their feelings in school, but as soon as they get out of school their anxieties and fears can be seen, but only if you look for them.

Since all of us had teachers like that, we often hear people say such things as "they might as well get used to it" or "I went through it and it didn't hurt me." Maybe it didn't hurt you, but it sure didn't help you either. We are not saying that teachers who shout will necessarily damage a child. Instead, we are saying that it can destroy the happiness of children for one or more years. Is there that much happiness in anyone's life that we can afford to throw away even a year of it?

Teachers and parents who shout should know right now that the feeling that the child has about you is embarrassment. Children can learn through rewards. There is nothing rewarding about being shouted at in front of a class.

Unfortunately, there is little that a parent can do about this. They can go up and see the teacher and tell her that she is making their child nervous. But communicating something like this to a teacher is a very delicate task. What you are basically saying is that she is not a very good teacher. If you complain to the principal, you have really started something.

An interesting experiment was recently done by some people at the State University of New York at Stony Brook. They looked at disruptive children in second and third grade classes. The teachers were found to shout at them a lot. These researchers then asked the teachers to soften their reprimands so that only the disruptive children heard them. When this happened, the amount of disruptive behavior dropped. Then they told the teachers they could get loud again, and the behavior of these children got worse. In other words, embarrassing a child by shouting at him in front of the class only makes him misbehave more. This is food for thought for parents *and* teachers.

We recently visited a Free School where the old rules were pretty much broken down. The children were at least as attentive and interested as in the regular school without any shouting or foolish rules on the part of the staff. Hopefully, some of these ideas from the Free Schools and the English schools will begin to filter down to the regular schools.

TRADITIONAL PSYCHOTHERAPY

Freud probably did more to make psychotherapy popular than did anyone else. People were interested in what Freud had to say, possibly because he talked about sex in a scientific way.

In those days, one usually did not talk about sex at all (although they probably did all of the same things that are done today), so this gave people a chance to talk about it in an intellectual manner. In Freud's psychoanalysis, you lay on a couch and said whatever came to your mind. After three or four years of this, you were supposed to figure out how to handle your problems better.

Because it took so much time, psychoanalysis was pretty much limited to the very rich. It is also a good deal for the analyst, because he can sit back, do very little, and, if you do not improve, it is your own fault. It had some advantages, though, which are beautifully caught in the title of Professor Schoefield's book on therapy, *Psychotherapy: The Purchase of Friendship.* Given the problems that most people have in relating to each other, therapy allowed the formation of deep relationships in the name of cure.

The time that psychotherapy takes led to the development of new techniques aimed at speeding the process up. For a while, one of the more popular approaches involved "Family Therapy," or what we call "Family Finking." In this approach, the family would sit around and accuse each other of things while the social worker acted as referee. Since most social workers only understand the middle class culture, this got to be quite a fiasco for many families.

Other types of therapies developed: Directive, nondirective, reality therapy, psychodrama, etc. Lately there are some new forms of therapy which, on the surface, appear to be more like parlor sex games than therapy.

Therapists are quite divided about what the goals of therapy should be, and for good reason. In the beginning, therapy was supposed to cure mentally ill people (in other words, people in mental hospitals or who should have been in mental hospitals but were too rich to commit[*]). Several research projects were done on its effectiveness. What these projects did was find the patients two or three years after discharge from the mental hos-

---

[*]See the works of Dr. Thomas Szasz for a fuller discussion of this.

pital or mental health clinic and see what happened to them. It was usually found that about two-thirds were able to adjust to the outside world after this amount of time. In some studies, they also looked at people who were supposed to go into mental health centers but could not get in because of overcrowding. Sometime later, sometimes as much as five years later, two thirds or more of these people were adjusted to the outside world. In other words, the cure rate seems to be the same whether or not you receive psychotherapy.

Now, therapists seem to talk about working with those little habits, fears, or quirks that annoy us or others. One wonders where it is all going. How can people be "cured" of those things when most live in urban centers which are too crowded, too impersonal, too competitive, and too dangerous to live in without developing some defenses? Can we ever achieve the perfectly balanced, cool, happy person? We doubt it.

Certainly, for the child who does poorly in school, talking about how he feels toward his mother and father will not make him a better student. Sometimes, though, giving him information about himself may relieve some of the child's anxieties. We remember one of our few successful attempts to talk a child out of his problems. He was a high school boy who read very poorly and was acting up because he was failing in school which, in turn, caused home pressures. When we explained (in about 15 minutes) that reading was just one skill which some youngsters have, and that there were other skills that *this* boy had, and that when he got out of school soon he could use his good skills with machinery, he bought it! He began to think of himself as a decent human being and felt little need to rebel against the school anymore. He developed, instead, a feeling of pity for the teachers who were trying to teach him things he could not learn. We, or somebody, should try this approach more often to see if it might have some potential.

BEHAVIOR MODIFICATION

Around the time of World War II, a Harvard psychologist, B. F. Skinner, began publishing his work in *shaping* behavior.

This work grew out of the *conditioning* experiments started by Pavlov. The principles were quite simple. When a person or animal does, on his own, something that we either want or don't want, we immediately *reward* him if it is "right" behavior, or punish him if it is "wrong" behavior. Given a certain number of such experiences, the person or animal either takes on the "right" behavior or stops *(extinguishes)* the "wrong" behavior.

Let us take an example to illustrate. Let us say that we want a hyperactive child to sit still. We set up a program wherein every time that child sits still for one minute, a machine pops out an M & M candy. Assuming that the child likes M & M's, he will force himself to sit still to get more of them. Soon the amount of time he has to sit still for a candy becomes two minutes. When he can do that easily, we push it up to three minutes, etc.

Many behavior modifiers believe that our personalities are formed by our reactions to rewards and punishments *(called positive and negative reinforcement)*. They feel that therapy should only deal with specific behaviors, and not with our basic personalities. For example, if you are afraid of heights, the *behaviorist* does not try to see what experience you had in the past to make you afraid of heights, but rather will attempt to *extinguish* the behavior (get rid of it) by a system of rewards and punishments. This works much faster and probably works at least as well as the old way of digging up your past.

There is no question that, for many children, this can work. Since it has been shown to work, more and more schools are importing behaviorists to take care of their problems. There are certain unanswered questions about this technique though:

1. Does it work? There is no real evidence in the research to show that it works for other than a few individuals who might have wound up improved anyway. There are many studies which show that one approach works for these three children, another experiment improved the behavior of those eight children, etc. But unless we know what would have happened to those children had their behavior *not* been modified, those few dramatic examples do us no good.

The way we find out about such things is by means of *control*

groups. This is the way it works. Let us say that we want to reduce the activity level of a group of children through behavior
modification. We call this the *experimental group.* We then find
two similar groups of hyperactive children who will be the control groups. In one control group, we may add a second teacher
or something like that to account for the fact that *something* is
being done for the experimental group (see discussion of Hawthorne effect, p. 96). So we do something for one control group.
We do nothing for the other control group. After the experiment is over, we compare the activity levels of the three groups.
Only if the experimental group is less active than both of the
other groups can we say that the behavior modification worked.
Because of the time, effort, and expense of this procedure, such
experiments are seldom carried out.

2. Even if the behavior modification group is better than
the other two groups in the example given above, a *cost-benefit*
analysis is seldom done. If a university professor comes in with
four graduate students to do the behavior modification program,
we must realize that, if the school had to pay for that help, the
program might have run 20 or 30 thousand dollars for a year,
compared to the $10,000 paid the extra teacher in one control
group, and the nothing extra paid for the other control group. In
terms of spending the educational dollar, we have to make a
decision whether the drop in hyperactivity shown by the experimental group is worth it. If, for example, we *could* accurately
measure activity level, let us say that the experimental group
dropped 25 percent in activity level while both control groups
only dropped 15 percent, suggesting that the time taken for the
experiment alone drops activity level by 15 percent. Now the
question is whether the 10 percent difference in activity level,
that is, the 10 percent better that the experimental group did,
is worth the ten or twenty thousand more that it cost.

3. There are many accounts of successful behavior modification in the scientific literature. We have seen many children
who were in such programs which had not worked. We wonder,
do these programs that *don't* work show up in the professional
journals? Obviously, the answer is no.

4. Let us say that we felt that the reduced activity level in

the classroom was due to behavior modification and was worth it. But what about other situations? Does the child whose activity level drops by ten percent more than expected in the classroom let all hell break loose when he gets *out* of the classroom? Does his activity level go up 20 percent in other classes or on the playground? No one knows at this time. We suspect that behavior modification acts quite specifically, so that it may work in that one classroom but, in terms of the child's overall behavior, will make no difference.

5. What are the long range effects? Some people see the handing out of rewards as a form of bribing. What does this experience do to their value system as adults? For example, one study of prostitutes found that one common thing in their background was the experience of being given things only when their behavior was right. We are not saying that behavior modification will set up a prostitute mentality in this society. On the other hand, we are not saying it won't.

6. There is an element of cruelty in the way that some behavior modification is done. For example, one lady came up to us after a lecture and told us that she had just finished a summer seminar in "behavior mod" at a large university. One day was spent in learning how to use an electric cattle prod. In some places, electric shock is used as the negative reinforcement to train children. Cattle prods or electric grids seem to be the favorite technique in some facilities for retarded children.

The "time-out" room is another. This is an empty room where the child is placed behind a closed door each time he displays a certain bad behavior. He may be put in there for one minute for the first offense, two minutes for the next time he does it, and ten minutes when he becomes a three-time loser. We have seen time-out rooms and it is amazing, given the poor reading skills of many children sent in there, the number of four and five letter words they can write on the walls. Sometimes we also wonder if the time-out room is such a new idea. When we were kids, we were sent to the clothes closet and, in those days of corduroy, the smell on a rainy day was really cruel and unusual punishment.

7. Some centers that practice behavior modification can get

to be a little too pure about the whole thing. Once this technique is brought into a school, some people can become very enthusiastic about it and try to modify almost everyone and everything around. For example, one behavior modifier we know who works in a hospital was so turned on about it that every time a problem came up he started setting up a program. One night some adolescent paraplegics got hold of some beer and one of them wound up throwing up. Our zealous friend wanted to "modify" the whole group out of drinking. Here were a group of youngsters whose backs were broken, who would never get out of a wheelchair, and were acting like adolescents. One could question the idea of interfering with their occasional fun.

Centers that use behavior modification sometimes act as if this technique and only this technique works and will refuse to consider others, such as drugs. We have encountered a couple of such places. We once evaluated a youngster who was being put in a home for bad boys. He was having rages that we felt would respond to anticonvulsant drugs. The school would not allow a trial with the drugs — their idea was that it was all bad habits. Another person had a very retarded and hyperactive child that took up the whole family's time and efforts. Rather than allowing him to be sedated at home, a day center for retarded children refused to take him unless all medication was stopped. In order to get a day training program for their child, this family *had* to deal with a nonstop bundle of impulses at home.

8. Some programs just aim too high. One of the main causes of this may be the teaching programs in the universities and workshops. In order to do *any* kind of therapy with children, one must first have a good knowledge about normal child development and exceptional children. It probably does very little good to set a behavior modification goal for a child if the child is physically too immature to do it. All too often, behavior modification seems to aim at hurrying maturity up. There is some question whether you can make the body grow faster through behavior modification. For example, we recently encountered a center for retarded children that had a behavior modification program. The child we knew was being trained to do something

that he just did not have the coordination to do. It was as frustrating to that child as daily ballet lessons would be for most of us. In fact, it turned out to be nothing more than teasing because they were always holding out rewards but the child could never get them. Like all teased children, he became cranky and miserable to live with.

9. To our mind, the main problem has to do with the idea behind behavior modification. First of all, if this technique would or could be successful, there are some frightening implications. Besides the fact that it could be used to push children into behaving abnormally, it could hide the main problem. As we have pointed out in other places, the problem is often not the child but rather the situation in which he finds himself. Zeroing in on the child can hide some of the bigger problems at home or in the school.

This raises all kinds of philosophical questions, such as does the end justify the means, how can we get humanitarian goals into education, etc.

Recently, B. F. Skinner, the main force in behavior modification, has suggested that people in our society have too much individual freedom and that this should be cut down through behavior modification. The implications of this horrible statement boggles the mind.

But, in fact, this is exactly what *does* happen in the school. If a child decides that he does not really care if he reads, and a behavior modification program is brought in, he may be in trouble. Let us say that this program gives him tokens for each successful reading experience, and that when he earns a certain number of tokens he can go outside and play (this is not unusual for a behavior modification program). If this child cannot, or will not, read, the only area of school in which he encounters success or enjoyment may be taken away from him. But basically the behavior modification people have come in and have *inflicted* their values and styles on the child. There is *no* choice. Conform or suffer. Can we be sure that the people running such programs have the right idea all the time as to what is proper behavior? Where is the child's right of appeal?

There is one good thing about behavior modification which does not get done nearly often enough. What behavior modification programs can do is act as a reminder to the teacher to reward children more often. There is never enough reward and almost always too much punishment in the schools.

JAILING CHILDREN

Books could be written on this subject and have. Some authors are outraged, but too often the way in which we jail children is hidden under the guise of "social welfare." As far as we can see, the only people whose welfare is benefitted from throwing children into jail are the people whose jobs are dependent upon keeping these prisons open.

Children are jailed for many reasons, some of which were mentioned on pages 144-146. But most of all, it is poor children who are jailed, and this has been true throughout American history. One of the most important events in the whole movement was the Irish immigration. The number and size of homes, centers, and other facilities which are nicely named jails increased tremendously to hold the Irish, whose main sin was being poor. We believe in our hearts that rich children then or today got off for the same crimes that the poor ones get sent up for.

Talking of jailed chilren, from our personal experiences, here is just part of a list of horror stories that originated in jails:

The eight-year-old boy who was disfigured when the oven he was cleaning at 5 A.M. exploded.

The two sisters, eight and ten, who were told by the matron that their mother was killed. When they started to cry, one was put in the corridor and the other in the time-out room.

The thirteen-year-old boy who ran away from jail, was found at home, and hanged himself rather than go back.

The mother who told us that her son was kicked out of public school repeatedly for smoking. Finally he was sent to a home for emotionally disturbed children, where he is allowed to smoke.

The many cases we have encountered where parents were conned or coerced into giving up their children's and their own legal rights by overzealous welfare or corrections workers.

This should be enough. It depresses us to try to dredge up any more memories.

DRUGS IN THE TREATMENT OF CHILDREN WITH
BEHAVIOR PROBLEMS

During the 1950's, America got turned onto drugs. Tranquilizers were being popped like aspirin. This led to greater experimentation with drugs with hyperactive children in order to slow them down. Three groups of drugs are used with such children:

1. Tranquilizers: With the up-tight, anxious adult, tranquilizers slow them down by calming them. But, surprisingly, when given to hyperactive children these drugs often speed their behavior up until they are even more unmanageable than before. This is called the *paradoxical reaction* of the drug (speeding up the child instead of slowing him down). However, it is far from a rule that tranquilizers will make *all* hyperactive children even more hyperactive. Some children have a high activity level in the classroom, usually because first, they become anxious easily and, second, they are not doing well in class and that makes them anxious. These children are not truly hyperactive because their activity level drops when they are free from pressure. Such children will often do well on tranquilizers.

2. Stimulants: The amphetamines (or uppers, as they are called in the drug culture of the street) very often will show the paradoxical reaction and slow down hyperactive children. The thinking is that these pills affect the part of the brain that sorts things out. As you read this, there may be movement or noises in the room. You do not notice them because your brain, which is noticing the sound or movement, filters out these unimportant things so that you can concentrate on the important thing of this moment, reading. In the hyperactive, distractible child, this filter is not working well. The stimulants may be making this brain center work better so that the distracting things are filtered out.

3. The anticonvulsants: As pointed out in several places in this book, the idea of the seizure — or convulsion — is taking on new meaning. It seems that many behaviors which cause problems in children are very much like seizures, but without

the usual convulsion that we expect with a seizure. Sometimes these seizures can take the form of a rage, a stomach ache, bed-wetting, a headache, or an impulsive act, such as fire-setting or hitting out. Even dreams may be a form of seizure in all of us. The dream, like the seizure, seems to have the effect of discharging the extra electricity in the brain so that the brain reaches *homeostasis* — a physical balance. For this reason, when tranquilizers and amphetamines do not work, sometimes anticonvulsants will. Unfortunately, we know that there are almost always side effects from anticonvulsants, such a problems with the gums.

The thing is that no one really knows which drug to try with which child. Every child is an experiment, and typically the stimulants are tried first, then the tranquilizers (which, if they work, may drop interest in learning) and sometimes, if neither works, the anticonvulsant is tried.

How helpful the drugs will be is still open to question. We have seen them work dramatically on some children and worsen others. There are certain problems in figuring out whether to use them. First of all, what will the long term effects be?* Will it heighten the chance that the child will move to these and other drugs as a teenager? Then, one of the most common ways for a child to stop being hyperactive is to mature. That is, almost all of the behaviors which people say are caused by minimal brain damage are not uncommon behaviors at some age in a child's life. It is only the age at which we see it that it becomes a problem. For example, no one is surprised to see an impulsive two-year-old. A hyperactive four-year-old is no surprise. A rage at three years does not surprise us. It is only when these behaviors occur later that we call them problems. Thus, it seems fairly clear that children grow out of many of the more noticeable symptoms, but it is the fact that they have not grown out of them at a specific point in time which causes difficulties. In addition, the research is poor at this time. The study has not been done in which such impulsive or hyperactive children were

---

*Some recent research suggests that the use of these drugs may slightly slow down growth.

placed in a totally stress-free and comfortable situation at a young age and followed up at a later age. Do the usual behavior problems which are seen in hyperactive children at a later age still show up if they are not subjected to the stress of being viewed as a problem child?

So how does the teacher know when to tell the parent that she wants a psychological evaluation for the child, in the hope that the psychologist recommends drugs? And when should the parent agree to seek a physician* in the hope of getting drugs? This brings up to the big question.

TO DRUG OR NOT TO DRUG

We have learned several things in this book which lead to this question. First, there is *no* single definition of a behavior problem — everyone makes up his own. Second, demands being placed on children for conformity are almost always impossible to meet. Third, we are probably all brain injured, and act that way from time to time. Fourth, there is so little choice in the school curriculum that there is often little else to do with a trouble-making child. Fifth, the behavior should improve with time because the behavior is a matter of immaturity in certain behavioral areas. Sixth, if the child can stop seeing himself as a problem, he may grow up healthier, which makes taking a chance worthwhile.

We have recommended medication for many children. But in doing so, one must be very careful. There are often great pressures to do something — do anything — to make this child conform. But one has to be very careful.

Certainly, drugs are necessary for children who are suffering from some form of seizure which is destructive to himself or to others. Included would be convulsions or the child whose lack of impulse control results in his being a potential danger to himself or his classmates. However, this probably includes very few children. In our discussions with school teachers and our own clinical observations, we find that there are probably one

---

*In case a physician is contacted, make sure he frequently follows up the child to make sure that there are no physical side effects from the drug.

or two truly uncontrolled and disruptive children in every class in the primary grades. After that, the number drops off considerably. For example, in our experience as school psychologists for a school district of 10,000 children, each year only a couple of hundred children were referred to us or to other agencies because of severe school behavior problems. The *real* problems actually could be counted on the fingers of two hands. Certainly every teacher in the lower grades complains about overactive and boisterous children. However, as mentioned above, they tend to grow out of it. What remains is the real problem, which is the curriculum lock-step and the unrealistic demands placed upon children by parents and teachers. This environmental stress can cause children to act out. We certainly cannot ignore the effects of a stressful environment on behavior. We have enough clinical case studies in the German concentration camps, prisons, etc. to indicate that placing humans into a dehumanizing and stressful enviroment causes a breakdown in their behavior.

On the other hand, when reports are printed in newspapers that as many as *fifty percent* of children in some classes have been given medication by their physicians in order to control their school behavior, it is, of course, a crime. This is the typical approach toward the child who does not conform to our very narrow limits of acceptable behavior.

Thus, the question is not whether to drug or not to drug, because the first focus should be on the environment in which the drugging takes place. If the schools are truly day prisons for the young in which a lock-step curriculum and unrealistic demands are placed upon too many children, it should be no surprise to us if children act out. Attempting to medicate them so that they do not act out, without altering the environment, is just treating the symptoms while ignoring the disease. Our first focus should be on the questions of individual differences and expectation for conformity and achievement. If the boundaries of expectations in these areas are broadened, it may well be that some of the other problems will disappear spontaneously.

Thus, each teacher and parent should really ask himself over and over again, "Are drugs the only way?"

SOME NEW TECHNIQUES

In our society's desperate attempts to achieve behavioral conformity, our scientists are always looking for new ways to accomplish this goal. Some of these techniques are interesting, some are horrifying. Let us look at one of each. First, the horrifying one. The following is a report found in the April, 1972, *Phi Delta Kappan,* the journal for professional educators: "In late February, a Washington, D.C., School of Psychiatry professor reported that brain surgery is being revived for relieving anxiety and tension suffered by overactive children and depressed mental patients.

"Well over 100,000 persons have already been subjected to psychosurgery around the world, including 20,000 in England, perhaps 50,000 in America, and many more thousands in Canada," says Dr. Peter R. Breggin.

"Children are being submitted to psychosurgery, particularly at the University of Mississippi where O. J. Andy is operating on hyperactive children as young as age 5, Breggin says."

The March, 1973 issue of *Ebony* goes into even greater detail. But, imagine! Cutting into the brain to "cure" a child of maturing slowly!

The second technique of interest has to do with megavitamins. This is the giving of massive doses of vitamins to hyperactive and autistic children.

The work of Dr. Linus Pauling, whose research concluded that massive doses of vitamin C prevents colds, probably was the main impetus for research in this area. However, even before this, vitamin B_3 was used with schizophrenics. Cott's results in New York with young schizophrenics have claimed that the younger the child is at the beginning of treatment, the better his chance for improvement. Recent work with vitamins B_3, B_6, C, E, niacin and pantothenic acid has resulted in positive claims for treatment of behavioral problems, alcoholism and drug addiction.

Certainly, the reactions of professionals has not been favorable. Physicians, who typically receive no training in nutrition have, in some cases, been downright nasty about the use of megavitamins. One reason often mentioned is that overdoses of vitamin A can kill, and there are isolated reports of deaths in the last few years from too much vitamin A. The fact that several million have died in the same period from malnutrition should balance off this danger.

The research on megavitamins is probably more extensive than that which was done before the use of drugs with hyperactive children was begun in many centers. Vitamin pills are much cheaper than drugs, probably have fewer adverse side effects, and probably are better for you. One wonders if these factors were taken into consideration, since it is quite probable that some vitamins will only be available by prescription in 1974, thus putting the cost out of reach of those who may need them most.

On a personal level, we have seen the use of megavitamins work in individual cases, but not in all cases, with colds, gum problems, headaches, etc. It certainly requires a long, careful look.

CHAPTER IX

ATTEMPTS TO DEAL WITH BEHAVIOR AT HOME

PREDICTING LATER BEHAVIOR

W E CANNOT predict the future. The best prediction for future behavior is present behavior. For example, children who do best on math tests as high school seniors tend to have scored their best in the arithmetic part of their third grade achievement test. We can say that a child who has good reading readiness in kindergarten has a higher chance of being a good reader later on than does a child with poor reading readiness skills. But we always know that there is always going to be one little rascal who won't do as we expect him to do.

People who have mental problems as adults often have a history of maladjustment in the past. But it does not necessarily follow that children who are seen as maladjusted in childhood will have mental problems as adults. Oftentimes, normal behavior of childhood is seen as maladjustment. A great deal depends upon the demands for conformity expected of a child. A relaxed, warm parent or teacher who enjoys children will see fewer children as maladjusted than a parent or teacher who does not like children.

For this reason, all we can do is talk about odds, much as we do when we talk about betting on horses. We can say that this child has a good chance of doing this, that that child will probably do that. Teachers, psychologists, and other professionals who deal with children can seldom, if ever, say a child *will* do something, without hedging bets a little bit. We can certainly say, with good assurance, that the retarded child *will not* graduate from college.* But we *cannot* say that he will not adjust well. In other areas, it is even less certain. Some clumsy children mature into ballroom dancers or athletes.

Since behavioral scientists are not successful at predicting the future, why do they try? An answer to this question might be "why indeed?" However, the demands for conformity in certain behaviors are so strong, it is sometimes helpful for parents and children to get the opinion of someone outside the family who is aware of the growth and development of children. This person can then hopefully give information to the parents and the school which can be helpful in understanding the child. For example, if parents have been expecting more school success from their child than the child can achieve, information about the child's growth and development can help them be more realistic. It can also be helpful to the classroom teacher who may also expect too much.

There is no one successful method known for raising children. But there are some helpful hints which may make it more peaceful in the home. Unfortunately, many parents have been led to believe that "sparing the rod spoils the child" and will use physical punishment so often that it is not useful. Grandmothers of the past with their good common sense used to say "Don't hit him so much. You will make him sassy." An outside agency may provide parents with some common sense direction which will stop the war within the home or the school.

The child expert, then, is not successful in predicting the future, but can describe and give information about the present. Then realistic expectations can be set for the child. Stress can

---

*This is true only if the child is truly retarded. It must be understood that even some children called retarded really are not. Tests given before the age of four are notoriously unreliable in measuring a child's school potential. At that age, some children are still so immature that one can't tell. We know, for example, a boy who could hardly talk at the age of four. He just had not learned how yet. He would have looked retarded on a test that required verbal answers. He was left alone, developed speech during his fourth year, and wound up being an above average student. Another person we know spoke Spanish as a child and was called retarded by the school. Luckily, he had a talent for languages and learned English as a second language quite easily. He has now completed all of his course work for a doctorate degree.

be reduced, and an improvement in the child's behavior often results.

There are a couple of other reasons why knowing more about the child can help in the long run:

1) It tells us with whom we have to be especially careful. The child with problems needs to have educational programs set up which cause him the least stress possible. The child who likes a challenge will probably continue to like one, as long as the challenges have a good chance of success and he does not get beaten down with failure. In other words, some long range planning *is* possible.

Most new and expensive programs in school are aimed at the older children, because when they act up it is much more noticeable. But new programs should be aimed at younger children. By the time they are at fifth or sixth grade level, it is probably too late to go back and undo all the harm we have done to them in the early years. Since we can know about children at a young age, we should aim to set up success experiences for them at that time.

2) The fact of the consistency of human behavior raises some important questions about our educational programming. Should we be working on the weakness of children, as we do in most remedial programs, or should we be working on their strengths? From this information, it looks like working on their weaknesses is our poorest bet, while working on their strengths is the best bet. If a child likes to tinker and does not like to read, forcing him to read has little chance of making a reader out of him. Letting him learn by doing seems to make more sense since there is a greater chance that he will always like to work with things.

Even though human behavior is fairly consistent, we must repeat that it is not a sure thing. No one — not psychologists, psychiatrists, social workers, nor your sister-in-law — can tell exactly who will have problems when they grow up.* Certainly,

---

*There are some studies which bear this out. Typically, for example, they might ask psychiatrists, psychologists, social workers and untrained aides in a mental hospital about how well they think people will adjust after discharge. All

if a child is severely retarded or profoundly psychotic by the time he reaches school age, it seems a sure thing. But beyond those very few children there are always a few surprises in the hopper.

There are always some problems that children grow out of, or at least that time changes. Shyness, for example, usually looks different in an eight-year-old than it does in a 28-year-old. We learn to hide some of our characteristics that make us uncomfortable. But they're there.

HOW CAN YOU BE A PERFECT PARENT?

There is no such thing as the perfect parent. Adults are human too. In order to be perfect, the parent would have to be like a computer. Only a computer can look at a problem without emotion and decide which action seems best at the moment. Parents are not computers. Parents have hang-ups, weaknesses, poor logic and everything else that goes into making one a human being. Hopefully, one other thing about most parents is that they are too blinded by love for their child to ever act with total logic in any given situation.

Many, if not most, parents cannot help the way they treat their children any more than the children can help the way they achieve in school. In our minds, the only way to improve the way a parent deals with their youngsters is to give them information. Certainly, all the pressures that parents are under to make their children compete in school, on the athletic field, and socially does not help the parent-child relationship. If the parent knows what to expect of the child, the parent may not lean on the child to the point that they both hate each other.

Books that tell parents how to act in order to be a perfect parent are way off base. We were watching a family recently that was a good example of this. The father is poorly educated, conservative politically, but a bit flamboyant personally. These characteristics actually have helped him become rich because, in his

---

of them do very poorly in predicting. Interestingly, the aides, who spend most time with the patients, often do better than the professionals. (Aside to professionals: For this reason, *always* ask the parent and teachers about the child.)

business, a person with too much education is not trusted, and the others in that business tend to be politically conservative but rather colorful folk.

By being this kind of man, the father has been able to give his children many more things than he would have, had he become a laborer. But, in doing so, he does not spend much time with the kids. He is not, was not, and never will be a sensitive man. He would have to be hit in the face with something before he would notice it. We strongly doubt that anybody could teach this man how to be sensitive.

His children get in trouble but he is rich enough to usually get them out of it. Others who know him ask why he can't give his children more guidance. The reason is that he just *can't*. Basically, his kids are just like he is except they are richer than he was. About all one can say about this family is thank goodness they are white and crooked enough to stay off welfare; otherwise they *really* would be in trouble.

HOW SHOULD YOU TALK TO A CHILD?

Some of the best-selling books on how to be a good parent almost lay out scripts for conversations between children and adults. You say this, and he will answer that, so then you can say this.

We remember watching a friend do the "give them a choice" bit: "Do you want to go to sleep now or in five minutes?" he asked the child. "Neither" was the answer. "Upstairs!" he yelled, and another experiment was shot.

Some parents find they avoid talking to their children because, once given an opening, the child will never stop. Some children, especially adolescents, are naturally as self-centered as they are hungry. For parents to always give in to this need of children to talk about themselves may be action beyond the call of duty.* Children should talk to other children as well. If

---

*It is normal for teenagers often to turn away from their parents. There may be many reasons, such as they are too busy, they are interested in other things, or they are afraid their parents will disapprove. When asked if he talks to his teenagers, one of our friends replied, "Sure, they always ask me for the car keys."

a child just wants to chat, and the parent or teacher is busy, tell the child politely to find another child to chat with. You will *not* ruin a child by reserving some privacy for yourself.

On the other hand, cutting off communication with a child can be the most destructive thing that can happen to a parent-child relationship. Someday, hard as it is to believe, the child *will* grow up and probably be as interesting (or as boring) as you are. The parent might even find that he enjoys the child, if he listens to him — but only up to a point.

However, parents have a right to happiness, too. This includes the right to privacy. Some parents would probably get along better if they ever got a chance to talk to each other alone. Sometimes, it is good for the soul for parents to sit together and make obscene gestures in the direction of the children in the next room. Just as long as they don't see.

Parents have rights, too. If a child is being cranky, the parent should tell the child that he does not enjoy cranky conversations, and until the child is ready to talk pleasantly, it will not help to have too much conversation.

Some parents and teachers only talk negatively to the children. Instead of saying "Hello," it's "Did you hang up your coat?", "Take your seat," "Don't mess up the house." Who can like someone who acts like Jack Webb playing a top sergeant?

Sometimes, parents and teachers spend so much energy seeing that everyone obeys *every* rule, that they can forget it is a human being they are dealing with.

Parents and teachers should treat children like human beings, kind of like they want to be treated. This includes talking to the child like a human being but also having the child treat them like human beings. One reward the parent can give the child for respecting the parents is to respect the child.

We are reminded of some families by Sam Levenson's joke. He said that he had never tasted white meat. When, as a kid, chicken was served, his parents always got all the white meat. By the time he became a parent, the child-centered society was here and he had to give all the white meat to his kids.

One of the most awful spin-offs from psychoanalysis is

the fault-placing put on parents. Everything that goes badly for a child is his parents' fault in that the parents did not treat him right. Usually this means that the parents did not talk to him enough. This has led to parents thinking that what they say has a profound effect on the child. This probably isn't so. Parents can give direction when a child is young, and advice when older. But this should be aimed at giving the child information. Some will be accepted and some rejected. But if the parent sticks with it, he will have done his job. But parents must realize that they cannot shape their child's life unless the child *wants* his life shaped. Nor should the parent devote too much time to trying to give advice and direction. It is probably more efficient to wait until asked.

ON TELLING CHILDREN THE TRUTH

We are trying very hard in this book to stay away from using expressions which only confuse things. The reason we will look at *cognitive dissonance* is not because you have to know the phrase. Instead, we want you to be aware of what happens, so when it happens to you, you can understand it better.

Cognitive dissonance is what we hope is happening to you as you read this book. If you live by a set of facts, and somebody gives you a different set of facts on the same subject, three things can happen: You can accept the new facts if they seem *more* believable than the old set to you, you can reject them if they seem *less* believable to you, or you can become confused. Usually people become confused if the new set of facts seem as believable as the old set of facts.

Let us take an example. Let us say that you tell children that marijuana is harmful, that it will soften their brain, that it is addictive, or that it will lead to taking heroin. The children will believe this set of facts you give them.

Then, let us say that they run into someone who tells them that he has taken marijuana, he likes it, has no interest in hard drugs, smokes it only occasionally, is doing very well in school, and gets along fine with everyone. This is the new set of facts.

Probably the child will not believe this new set of facts. It is less believable than this present set of facts.

But then, let us say that he reads that his sports hero often blows pot, that national magazines say it is neither harmful nor addictive, and runs into other people who have taken it without any harm coming to them. Then we see cognitive dissonance.

He may become defensive — even fanatic — in denying these new facts so that he does not have to face the confusion. He may even become an informer, basing this on the idea he is saving his friends and at the same time he is able to live with his set of facts.

On the other hand, he may become angry with you for telling him lies. He may throw these new facts in your face very often. In doing so, he may seem very angry. He probably is not angry at first, as much as he is trying to figure out where the truth is. But if he figures eventually that you *did* lie, he may become very angry. Then, he will figure that, if you lied on that one thing, you have lied on other things and he does not believe you much on anything any more.

One can see cognitive dissonance appear on someone's face. Go to a meeting in the suburbs where some minority leader tries to tell the people why the minority people are angry. Most people will say something like, "There were some things that he said that were true, but I can't buy *all* that." They usually do not want to discuss the points logically, but are angry. They may become all the more prejudiced, or they may get to the point where they are more radical than the most radical minority leader.

In dealing with children, you are probably safer if you mostly tell them the truth. You can't tell them the *whole* truth. You can't tell *anybody* the whole truth. But you can duck answering rough questions when children are small, and when they are bigger they probably will know enough not to ask you.

The way you do this is to be realistic. Let's take the example of marijuana we talked about above. You can tell children that smoking marijuana is against the law. You can tell them that some people get thrown in jail and that jail is terrible. You can tell them that kids are usually caught by people they trust. You can tell them it is dangerous. If they press you about your feelings, you can duck the issue if you are afraid that what you say may lead the youngsters into trouble, and say something like "I don't know enough about it but I want to be sure that you don't get into trouble."

You can back this up by finding out about other things that will prove you right and telling your children things like:

Smoking is an addiction. Once most people start, they can no more stop than a junkie can stop using drugs.

Booze is something that adults do. It is against the law for kids to do it.

Premarital sex can be dangerous. First, the girl can become pregnant, so if they are going to do it, make sure they plan their sex. Romance is great, but babies ain't. Second, youngsters may mistake a sexual relationship for love and marry because of it. This is just as dangerous because then they can have babies legally. In our mind, it is a crime to have a baby if you cannot love it.

Shoplifting is against the law. Even if the youngsters feel that they are "ripping off some fat cat," some not-so-fat salesclerk may suffer.

And so on.

TEASING

Teasing children makes them cranky children. Just like holding a toy out to a baby and pulling it back before he can grab it may make him cry, teasing can make older children cranky.

Don't hold rewards out to them that you do not intend to give. Do not tell them you will do something that you do not intend to do. This doesn't mean you can't set conditions for them ("If you do this, I'll give you that") but be sure you are willing to keep your end of the bargain.

Do not tease them about their clothes, their friends, or their music. Either they will become cranky, or will tease back, and then you will become cranky.

WHY ARE CHILDREN LAZY? HOUSEHOLD CHORES

A friend of ours, a teacher, was remembering how he once goofed badly. He had a boy in his class who was doing poorly. At a parent conference, he told the widowed mother that the boy was just lazy. Imagine his shock when he found the mother laughing. Lazy? This boy was a ball of fire at home. He almost ran the whole house. He did all the chores plus going to school. How could anyone call him lazy?

There are two kinds of laziness in children. The first is seen in teenagers. Sometimes, the stress, the strain, and the physical changes that come at adolescence leave some children so short of energy that they can barely move, even for things they like.

But most children have a great deal of energy. Their only trouble is that they will not apply that energy to what *you* want.

There will be times that you will find it easier to do something yourself than to go to all the trouble of forcing a child to do a chore against his will. But children should feel some responsibility for helping around the house. Some useful hints:

1) Do not assign chores to your children when they are too young to do them. Tasks such as dishwashing, sweeping, etc., require a certain amount of coordination. If they are too hard for a child, let them go until the youngster matures enough so that handling a dishrag or a broom comes almost as easy to him as it does to you. Young children can do only chores which require the least coordination, like carrying out garbage or walking the dog.

2) Do not assign very small children (up to 8 or 9) any regular chores unless they are interested in doing them. Most young children will goof them up so badly that you will have to do them over anyway. Let them help when they volunteer. All too often, when they do volunteer, you will wish they were less interested.

3) Don't make the chores too routine. Children are not blessed with the interest, attention span, or motivation to do any task every day. Parents are forced into it because they are parents and have to keep the house up.

You're bound to lose if you try to push them into doing a

chore every day. Save chores until you really *need* help and you have a much higher chance of getting help. If you make children do routine chores, they will feel they have done their part and may fight you if you ask them to do something extra. For example, if you want to go out early some evening, and the kids have done nothing for a few days, you may get dishwashing, kitchen cleaning, garbage disposal, pet care, and whatever else you need, all in one night, and this may be more than you would get if you spread one routine chore over every day.

4) Chores do not build character. Youths who are lazy around their parents' house may do all right in their own home. A neat child may grow into a slob. Try to be flexible. When children go through their sloppy stage, you might as well adjust to it as much as you can. Most children go through it and trying to fight it is a losing battle. Make a deal with them: they clean their room when it really gets bad and in between times keep the bedroom door shut. If two share a room, and one is sloppy and one neat, divide the room and allow each of them to do their own thing in their half.

5) Some chores are so distasteful that you will have to be selective. In one home we know, the children *refuse* to go to the garbage rack to dump trash unless it is an emergency. There are, after all, all those icky spiders and bugs which may be around and who wants to run into them? For another child, making the bed may be just as distasteful. Trade off, or use it to your advantage. Sample technique for conning children:

Parent: Would you please dump the garbage?

Child: Ick! Bleck!

Parent: Oh, o.k. You do the dishes while I dump the garbage.

6) Don't be a sexist. Boys should learn how to take care of themselves as well as girls. Boys should know how to cook, sew, and clean. After all, if you're lucky, he will move out someday and will have to know this.

7) Say "please" and "thank you."

8) Let the child overhear you tell your friends what a fine help the child is around the house.

WHEN SHOULD YOU HIT A CHILD?

Traditionally, parents have hit their children when they feel like doing it. It has always been fascinating to us to watch parents go Christmas shopping with their children. They walk down aisles full of toys and the children reach for them. Small children can no more keep their hands off toys than a drunk can pass up a free one. Slap! Pow! Crack! the parents hit their children. Often, the parents do not even seem angry but are cracking them just out of habit.

Parents are hitting their children more and more. In New York City, reported child abuse went up over 500 percent in five years. It is estimated that over two million children are physically abused every year.

Recently, *The Wall Street Journal's* survey showed that 49 states allow spanking in school and there is a great increase in the number of teachers who want to have corporal punishment (belting children) made simpler. Fifty-seven percent of teachers are for use of the "board of education." In Pittsburgh, 73 percent of teachers signed a petition to lift a ban on spanking.

How can these people think, after four or ten years of the school turning children off, when a child has not had one success experience in what he sees as a day prison, and the child knows that he doesn't have the skills that the school wants, that one belt from a teacher will make a kid conform in behavior? To think that this type of punishment is going to have any long-range effect is downright stupid.

We know of one school where the principal made teachers "volunteer" to hold a child while he got whacked with a paddle in full view of the children in the office. Maybe this does get a child to conform for a few months but, in the long run, will probably get the kid to hate school all the more.

There is no evidence that hitting a child will change his behavior. Therefore, we must conclude that parents and teachers most often hit their children because it makes *them* (the adults) feel better rather than out of any misplaced concern for the child.

This is the most depressing part of the whole thing. If parents had a child (it does take two to have one) and realizes that they cannot keep from hitting a child because it makes the *parents* feel better, he or she should run right down and get sterilized before committing the crime of having more children.

If a teacher lays hands on a child in anger because it makes the *teacher* feel better, someone should remind the teacher that he is earning somewhere between six and twenty thousand a year to work with children. If all this money doesn't make him feel good enough, and he has to brutalize children for his own comfort, he should retire or be retired from teaching.

Teachers should *never* hit a child except in self-defense. The teacher would probably do better to spend his energies on changing the school curriculum so children are interested in what they are doing. A recent Gallup Poll showed that twice as many parents and teachers are interested in the child's deportment than care about his curriculum. To our mind, that's a flip-flop in values.

In an emergency, or when under a lot of stress, a parent might strike a child. But this should be such a rare happening that both the parent and the child remember it.

The main thing about spanking is, of course, that the more you do it the less effective it is. If a parent hasn't struck a child for let's say two years, and the child commits a real bad sin, so bad that the parent slaps the child once, this will have more effect than the brass knuckles treatment will have on children who get it every day.

Our observations are that most spankings are given to children who are acting quite naturally for their age. Hitting a five-year-old for yelling or a four-year-old for not being able to sit still is like throwing a teenager in jail for feeling romantic.

In some societies children are never hit and act quite nicely. Hitting a child will probably result in his hitting other children often (and getting hit by his parents for hitting other children) and in his becoming generally surly and nasty. Look around your neighborhood and you will probably notice that the child who gets beaten most often is *still* the worst actor on the block.

As one educator was quoted in *The Wall Street Journal*, paddling ". . . is a revolting manifestation of intellectual and professional bankruptcy."

WHAT HAPPENS TO A CHILD WHEN THE PARENTS ARE DIVORCED OR THE MOTHER WORKS?

If only we had a nickel for every time a teacher has contacted us about a "problem" child and ended up with "Well, what do you expect? The mother works." Or, confidentially, "The parents are separated, you know."

Once, after being hit with it for the third time in one day in one school, we did a count of the number of teachers who had school-aged children. Almost all of them did. Were almost all of their children having problems? Quite probably not.

Other studies have looked at the families of children to see if there are any differences between divorced families and those that stay together. One thing that always messes up this kind of research is how rich the family is. Poor children have more trouble in school than do rich children (see pp. 000-00). Rich and middle-class parents more often stay married because they do not have the pressures of earning enough to eat, they are more conforming to the society because they feel *part* of society, the welfare system — which encourages divorce and desertion — does not affect them, and their jobs often offer outlets for satisfaction outside the home so that they are better able to stand going home.

But not considering the money angle, research shows that it doesn't make much difference in children's school achievement or behavior whether the parents are married, divorced, separated, widowed, or have been a single parent and later married. The only condition that seems to negatively affect the children's performance in school is if the parents do not like each other and stay together for "the sake of the children."

One laboratory for research on the effects of the "right" kind of family has been the Israeli Kibbutz. Here, children are raised in nurseries and only see their parents for a couple of hours a day. Research shows that these children are no better or no worse adjusted than those who are raised by their families.

In their 1961 study of 400 persons of eminence throughout history, *Cradles of Eminence*, the Goertzels found that 190 of these men and women had fathers who were failures or alcoholic.

In 351 of the cases, conditions in the home life of these people caused unhappiness in them.

The myths about working or divorced mothers die hard. But as more and more families use legal means to get out of tough situations, maybe people will stop pointing a finger at the mother. And it is mother who gets the finger pointed at her, rather than the father. Maybe that is because most of the authorities who, in their books, point fingers at mother, are men.

BAD FRIENDS

Certain children are just naturally liked more than others. Children tend to form into groups and, like in herds of chimpanzees, one or two children seem to be at the center of the group. Other children tend to be isolated by their playmates.*

In the neighborhood, it is the closeness of other children which is often the first factor in the selecting of friends. If the parents leave them alone, children will tend to find their best friends among those who have the most similar interests. The immature child will tend to play with younger children, quiet children will tend to stick together, and the neighborhood bullies are usually allies, except when their rivalry interferes.

In school, children usually select their friends in the same way while young. However, as they get along in the grades, school achievement comes into play. The better students will stick together. Since the teacher and/or grading system always makes them aware of who is a troublemaker or poor student, these outcasts are usually thrown together.

As children get older, familiarity becomes important. Children who were friends while young may stay that way, even though their interests take their own path.

It is doubtful that "bad" friends make a child into a bad child. Rather, they will tend to come together more out of common interests or old-times' sake. In the first case, the child who has a poor self-image will join other losers. If he can be made to see himself as a worthwhile individual, he will probably abandon

---

*This should not be confused with the disruption and misery caused by some over-controlling parents in trying to set up their children's social lives.

his "evil companions." If it is the second case, and your child's old friend has "gone bad," the chances are that they will do little together. However, there is always the chance in both cases that a child may accidently get pulled in on trouble.

But that is a calculated risk that must be taken. Forcing a child to give up friends can only be done through subtle persuasion, rather than with a club. Even then, if you push too hard (and most adults do), the child will probably become very stubborn and remain loyal to a friend he may not even like. It is usually best to allow such relationships to die of natural causes.

THE GENERATION GAP

Kids today yell that their parents do not understand them. The young claim that their parents are too hung up to dig where it's all coming from (translation for parents "too hung up to dig where it's all coming from": their parents don't understand the subtle nuances and implications of their children's philosophical stance).

On the other hand, the parents whisper to each other "Don't trust anyone under 30." This is called the generation gap.

The real generation gap actually started with the last generation. When the boys came home from The War to Save Democracy (we believe it was the Second World War that was supposed to do that), they threw off the old ways. They dressed in tee shirts and khakis, played with their kids, and acted young. Before that, as soon as a youngster reached adulthood (took a job), even if they were eight years old at the time, they dressed like adults and tried to act like they thought adults should act. The War ended that and it is amazing to think that the rebels of the 40's are today's conservatives. But the chances are that the young adults of the late 1940's were more different from their parents than any generation before or after.

Today's parents have put the "gap" label on their own children's behavior. At times, it seems that the older generation has declared war on their own children. Many parents have very short memories of when they were young. In their thinking, they never made mistakes, were always obedient, kind, trustworthy, cooperative, hard-working, etc. "What's wrong with the kids today?" is the battle cry.

It is interesting sometimes to listen to parents in relaxed moods telling stories of the "pranks" they did when young. Falsifying I.D. cards to get liquor under age, joyriding in cars (stealing now), halloween jokes (property damage now), sexual experiences during the war (new morality now), playing hooky (truancy now), are among the common memories of many.

Every generation of parents has moaned and complained about "the kids of today." Complaints about kids are found in the writings of the earliest civilization at Sumer and in the words of the ancient Greek Philosopher, Socrates. Nothing much really changes.

But since World War II, parents have had much more time to spend with their children, and, unfortunately, to get involved in their children's lives. Childhood gets longer and longer. Not too many years ago, when most children ended school at eighth or ninth grade, childhood ended. A working boy of 14 or 15 was not seen as a child. Today we read or hear about the youth movement and people of 21 to 27 years of age called "the kids." Many young people of college age and older are treated by their parents as children.

The hopes and dreams for "the children" become more important than the parents' own happiness. When so much is hoped for the children, disappointment is often unavoidable. Young people will always live somewhat differently than the last generation and will also want to make their own mistakes. The generation gap can widen when parents are too eager to control their children's lives. It is resented as much by young people as it is by us when grandma and grandpa are too free with advice.

The job of parents is to protect and guide a young child until he is able to control and protect himself. But parents must learn when to let the child begin to make decisions. There are mothers and fathers who still remind sixteen and seventeen-year-olds to wash their hands and face. Unless the child's development is very slow indeed, this type of parental direction is ridiculous. If in sixteen or seventeen years the youngster has not yet learned these simple tasks, further instruction won't help.

Older people often feel that it is perfectly all right to be rude to young people. Yet the complaint is always heard of how rude young people are. It is our feeling that young people have good models for rudeness when we listen to what older people say to them. Notice how many times sales people, relatives and neighbors make rude, personal remarks about the physical appearance of youngsters, ranging from "Why don't you cut your hair?" to "Why do you wear that outfit?" Our feelings would be hurt if someone made remarks like that to us. Can you imagine a youngster saying to an adult in a store "Your heels are run down, why don't you get them fixed?" or "You wear so much makeup you look like a clown." We would be shocked. Yet many people feel free to criticize the appearance of any young person whether they know him or not.

Children rarely grow up to be the perfect people their parents wanted; not in this generation nor in the last generation. Once a parent realizes this, he will not be nearly as disappointed. As children grow into their teen years, parents should practice a policy of "benign neglect" and remember that each generation does grow up eventually. You may still worry about their safety, but the less you interfere, the better your mental health will be.

Reading their mail, listening in on their phone conversations and searching their rooms may be exciting fun, but will do little to establish trust or change their behavior. And there is always the terrible possibility that you may learn something that will cause you needless worry and concern.

There is indeed a generation "gap." There has to be. Each generation has a gap in age between it and the next. The "gap" between the teenager and his parents is no wider than the gap between the parents and the grandparents. The "gap" does not have to mean lack of love and respect, but it frequently does mean a difference in interests, values and life plans. It can be very exciting to live with a member of the "now" generation, especially when you realize that in a very short time they will be asking you, "What's wrong with the kids today?"

CHAPTER X

A FINAL PLEA

R ECENTLY WE attended a meeting. Some wealthy parents were
looking at a private school for their child and what did we
think of it. We were very negative to the school administrators.
One selling point was that this school could provide remedial
reading. But, so what, we asked, since remedial reading doesn't
work very well anyway.

Well, the school administrators replied, one parent just wrote
us that their boy, who was nine and reading at first grade level
when he started with us, is now 14 and reading at ninth grade
level. So what, we asked, since we have heard that story many
times and yet in the thousands of children we've seen we have
never seen it happen to *one* of them that we've tested, no matter
how much tutoring they have gotten.

Well, they replied, we have small classes. But, so what, we
asked, since classes are boxes into which we put children for
administrative convenience, not to teach them.

Well, they replied, some of our children get back into the
public schools and some even go on to college and are very
successful. So what, we asked, since we have encountered many
successful people who stumbled through college and went into a
field which required little reading, or their father bought a building for a college and they got through that way, or they were
very good verbally so they bluffed and talked their way through
school.

Well, they replied, we will be nice to the children. Ah! Now
you're talking, we said. It's protection money. The parents will
pay so that you are nice to the child. *That* makes practical sense.

Later, the parents cornered us in the hall. Why, they asked, can't some of the things you propose be done in the public schools? We both became very downcast.

First of all, we replied, from our limited experience, it seems that if we *really* want change — true change — in the schools, we probably should shut them down and start all over again. The system is like a big sponge. You throw a new idea into it and — slurp! — it's sucked into the middle and by the time you squeeze it out the idea has been dirtied too much by the other things in the sponge to be palatable.

Secondly, society is misusing the schools. Given a high unemployment rate, we have to do something to limit the labor force. So we keep kids in school longer. By doing this, without changing the schools, we frustrate them and guarantee that a large number of them are failures.

Thirdly, money always has to be the answer. Now, we do not agree that more money is needed for education. On the other hand, we do not disagree. Who knows? The thinking seems to be that if we spend a certain amount on education, and it doesn't work very well, by spending more on the same old thing, we *will* make it work well. That, obviously, is false. Possibly, if we spent more of the money now being spent, but spent it in different ways, the cost effectiveness would be greater.

Finally, there is the fact that the room we had just left was full of guilty parents and teachers. They are guilty because they have been brainwashed into being dissatisfied with their children. Because, by one definition, the schools fail with 85 percent of the children, it seems a little foolish to be unhappy if you are in this great majority. In our wild drive for sameness, we have wasted some beautiful skills and talents in our children.

What can we do, they asked. Subvert from within was the answer. Agitate for realistic change. Fight credentialism. Utilize, instead of trying to eliminate, individual differences. And love your children.

FURTHER READINGS

The following references do not necessarily relate directly to the text. Rather, they are suggested readings for persons who would like to pursue a subject further.

Chapter Three

Blodgett, Harriet: *Mentally Retarded Children: What Parents and Others Should Know.* Minneapolis, U of Minn. Press, 1971.

Cronbach, Lee: *Essentials of Psychological Testing.* New York, Harper Brothers, 1949.

Deloria, Vine: *Custer Died for Your Sins: An Indian Manifesto.* New York, MacMillan and Company, 1969.

Herskovits, Melville J.: *The Myth of the Negro Past.* Boston, Beacon Press, 1941.

Noar, Gertrude: *Sensitizing Teachers to Ethnic Groups.* Anti-Defamation League of B'nai B'rith, distributed by Allyn & Bacon, New York.

Silberberg, N.E., Iversen, I.A. & Silberberg, M.C.: A model for classifying children according to reading level. *J. Learning Disabil., 2* (12):634-642, 1969.

Silberberg, N.E. & Silberberg, M.C.: Hyperplexia: The other end of the continuum. *J Spec. Edu., 5* (3):233-242, 1971.

————:A late—but indignant—comment on the arguments raised by Jensen. *School Psychol., 24* (4):37-40, 1970.

————: Reading rituals. *Transaction, 8* (9-10):45-49, 1971.

Stroud, James B.: *Psychology in Education.* New York, David McKay, 1956.

Thompson, Lloyd J.: Language disabilities in men of eminence. *J. Learning Disabil. 4:*39-50, 1971.

Wyatt, Susan: *The Mark: A Case for the Abolition of Grading.* Washington, D.C., Center for Educational Reform (2115 S. Street Northwest.)

Chapter Four

Ames, Louise Bates: *Is Your Child in the Wrong Grade?* New York, Harper & Row, 1966.

————: *Stop School Failure.* New York, Harper & Row, 1972.

Bowles, Samuel: Getting nowhere: Programmed class stagnation. *Society,* 9:42-49, 1972.

Diamond, Daniel & Bedrosian, Hrach: *Industry Hiring Requirements and the Employment of Disadvantaged Groups.* New York, N.Y.U. School of Commerce, 1970.

Furth, Hans: *Piaget for Teachers.* Englewood Cliffs, N.J., Prentice Hall, 1970.

Goins, Jean: *Visual Perceptual Abilities and Early Reading Progress.* University of Chicago Supplementary Educational Monographs #87, 1958.

Greer, Colin: *The Great School Legend.* New York, Basic Books, 1972.

Iversen, Iver; Silberberg, N.E. & Silberberg, M.C.: Sex differences in knowledge of letter & number names in kindergarten. *Percept. Mot. Skills, 31:*79-85, 1970.

Kramer, S.N.: *History Begins at Sumer.* Garden City, N.Y., Doubleday, 1959.

Ribich, Thomas I.: *Education and Poverty.* Washington, D.C., The Brookings Institute, 1968.

Silberberg, N.E.; Silberberg, M.C. & Iversen, I.A.: The effects of kindergarten instruction in alphabet and numbers on first grade reading. *J. Learning Disabil.,* 5(5):254-261, 1972.

Silberberg, N.E. & Silberberg, M.C.: Myths in remedial education. *J. Learning Disabil.,* 2 (4):209-217, 1969.

Stephens, J.M.: *The Process of Schooling: A Psychological Examination.* New York, Holt, Rinehart & Winston, 1967.

Chapter Five

Henry, Jules: *Culture Against Man.* New York, Random House, 1963.

Huey, Edmund: *The Psychology and Pedagogy of Reading.* Cambridge, MIT Press, 1968 (reprinted from 1908 MacMillan edition.)

Katz, Michael: *Class, Bureaucracy and Schools: The Illusion of Educational Change in America.* New York, Praeger, 1971.

Silberberg, N.E. & Silberberg, M.C.: The bookless curriculum: An educational alternative. *J. Learning Disabil.,* 2 (6):302-307, 1969.

————: Is there such a thing as a learning disabled child? *J. Learning Disabil.,* 4 (5):273-276, 1971.

————: An open letter about a dyslexic man, *Minn. Reading Quarterly* 15 (1):5-8, 1970.

Chapter Six

Birch, Herbert & Gussow, Joan: *Disadvantaged Children: Health, Nutrition and School Failure.* New York, Harcourt, Brace & World, 1970.

Ehrenreich, Barbara & Ehrenreich, John: *The American Health Empire.* New York, Random House, 1970.

Kawi, A. & Pasamanick, Benjamin: *Pre-Natal and Para-Natal Factors in the Development of Childhood Reading Disorders.* Monographs of the Society of Research in Child Development, 1959.

Leslie, Loren: Prematurity as an etiological factor in cerebral dysfunction. *Arch. Phys. Med. Rehab.,* 47:711-714, 1966.

Robey, James, Blyth, Carl and Mueller, Frederick: Athletic injuries: Application of epidemiologic methods. *JAMA,* 217:184-189, 1971.

Scott, Jack: *The Athletic Revolution.* New York, The Free Press, 1971.

Chapter Seven

Goertzels, Victor and Goertzels, Mildred: *Cradles of Eminence*. Boston, Little Publishing, 1962.

Silberberg, N.E. and Silberberg, M.C.: *Glue Sniffing in Children: A Position Paper*. Sister Kenny Institute, mimeographed.

————: School achievement and delinquency, *Rev. Educ. Res., 41*(1):17-33, 1971.

Szasz, Thomas: *The Myth of Mental Illness*. New York, Harper & Row, 1961.

Chapter Eight

Graber, David: Megavitamins, molecules and minds, *Hum. Behav.*, 2:8-15,

Levine, Murray and Levine, Adeline: *A Social History of Helping Services*. New York, Meredith, 1970.

Mason, B.J.: Brain surgery to control behavior, *Ebony*, March 1973.

Silberberg, N.E. and Silberberg, M.C.: Should schools have psychologists? *J. School Psychol.*, 9(3):321-328, 1971.

Chapter Nine

Festinger, L.: *A Theory of Cognitive Dissonance*. Stanford, Stanford University Press, 1957.

NAME INDEX

211

SUBJECT INDEX

213